PageMaker

DESIGN TECHNIQUES

For Windows

PageMaker

DESIGN TECHNIQUES

For Windows

Michael J. Nolan

with

Rick Gregory & Abbo Peterson

Hayden Books
Indianapolis , Indiana

International Standard Book Number: 1-56830-022-0
Library of Congress Catalog Card Number: 93-78060

96 95 94   4 3 2 1

Interpretation of the printing code: the rightmost double-digit number is the year of the book's printing; the rightmost single-digit number is the number of the book's printing. For example, a printing code of 94—1 shows that the first printing of the book occurred in 1994.

Printed in the United States of America

Trademark Acknowledgments

There are too many trademark acknowledgments to list on one page. To acknowledge every product and every company would require that we double the size of this book. However, because we are environmentalists, and because paper is a valuable (and costly) commodity, we are limiting our trademark acknowledgments to the following statement:

All products mentioned in this book are either trademarks of the companies referenced in this book, registered trademarks of the companies referenced in this book, or neither. We strongly advise that you investigate a particular product's name thoroughly before you use the name as your own.

Published and distributed to the trade by Hayden Books, a division of Prentice Hall Computer Publishing. For sales information, address Hayden Books, 201 W. 103rd St., Indianapolis, IN 46290, or call 1-800-428-5331.

About the authors

In 1986, Michael J. Nolan co-founded one of the country's first totally-electronic design studios in San Francisco, PRINTZ Electronic Design. PRINTZ's expertise in the design and production of print and multimedia was soon recognized by a large corporate clientele. PRINTZ continues to lead in the application of new technologies. Michael is currently Director of Art and Design for Prentice Hall Computer Publishing in Indianapolis, Indiana.

Abbo Peterson became involved in desktop publishing and was able to combine his interest in photography and personal computers when he started work at Aldus Corporation in 1987 as a software support technician. His keen interest in customers' needs, sense of visual design, and attention to detail have allowed him to provide valuable feedback during product development. Abbo has been the Macintosh PageMaker Product Specialist at Aldus since 1992 and was heavily involved in the development of PageMaker 5.0.

Rick Gregory has been involved with computers for the past 15 years. Rick merged his interest in computers with his interest in design and visual arts when he joined Aldus in 1990. He worked for two years as a software support technician helping users with PageMaker, FreeHand, and PhotoStyler. Rick's background in desktop color issues enabled him to provide feedback during the product development cycle on the separation and color features that are new to PageMaker 5.0. In 1992, Rick became the Windows PageMaker Product Specialist.

Credits

Publisher
David Rogelberg

Acquisitions Editor
Marj Hopper

Editors
Karen Whitehouse
Matt Ciskowski

Imprint Manager
Scott Cook

Designer
Michael J. Nolan

Design Assistant
Barbara Webster

Photographer
Don Distel,
Spahr Photography

Production Analyst
Mary Beth Wakefield

Proofreading/Indexing Coordinator
Joelynn Gifford

Graphics Image Specialists
Dennis Sheehan
Joe Ramon

Indexer
Jeanne Clark

We want to hear from you

We value your opinions, because our success at Hayden depends on what you think of our books. If you have any comments, no matter how great or how small, we'd appreciate your taking the time to send us a note, by whatever means you prefer.

We can be reached at the following address:

David Rogelberg, Publisher
Hayden Books
201 W. 103rd St.
Indianapolis, Indiana 46290

(800) 428-5331 voice
(800) 448-3804 fax

E-Mail:
America Online   Hayden Bks
AppleLink   hayden.books
CompuServe   76350,3014
Internet   HaydenBks@aol.com

Introduction

Aldus PageMaker, introduced in 1985, revolutionized the graphic arts industry. It freed designers from laborious paste-up tasks, enabling them to make layout changes in minutes that formerly would have taken hours or days. Most importantly, it allowed instantaneous feedback on design decisions. Being able to immediately see and refine ideas on screen or on paper is perhaps the greatest advantage of electronic design technology.

PageMaker is a very intuitive software program—relatively simple to learn. Graphic design and production processes are not as easily understood, and that's where this book is designed to help. The intention here is to bridge the knowledge gap that exists between utilizing PageMaker and understanding how it applies to the creation of beautiful publications.

This book assumes you already have a working knowledge of PageMaker. It is organized in a non-linear fashion so you can begin anywhere and learn what you need to know. Like Chess, you can learn PageMaker's basic moves in a few minutes; it takes longer to become an expert. It is our hope that *Design Techniques* will be a guide for you as you develop and enhance your graphics skills.

Contents at a glance

Contents

PART II: TYPE

Fonts

Specifications

Spacing

Importing

Headlines

Initial caps

Indents/tabs

Pull Quotes

Rules and underlines

Styles

Story editor

Text blocks

Hyphenation

Contents

This section introduces you to design and production concepts using Aldus PageMaker. What follows is a wealth of information about the features, characteristics, and tools to create outstanding and provocative designs.

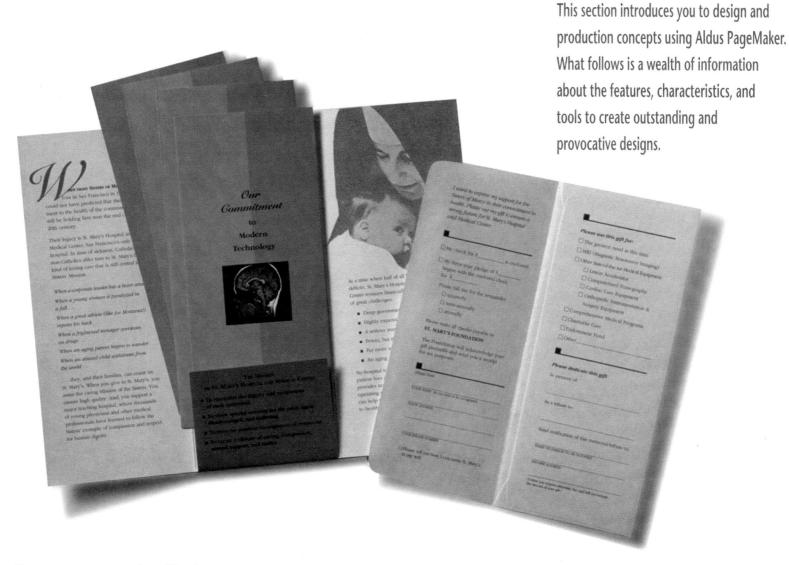

The many components of a publication are seen here in this package.
Designer: Deborah Reinerio, Red Hot Designs,
San Francisco
Client: St. Mary's Hospital Foundation

This newsletter mockup, using Lorem Ipsum, "greek text", displays the different elements of a typical document. Study the spread closely if you are unfamiliar with layout terminology.

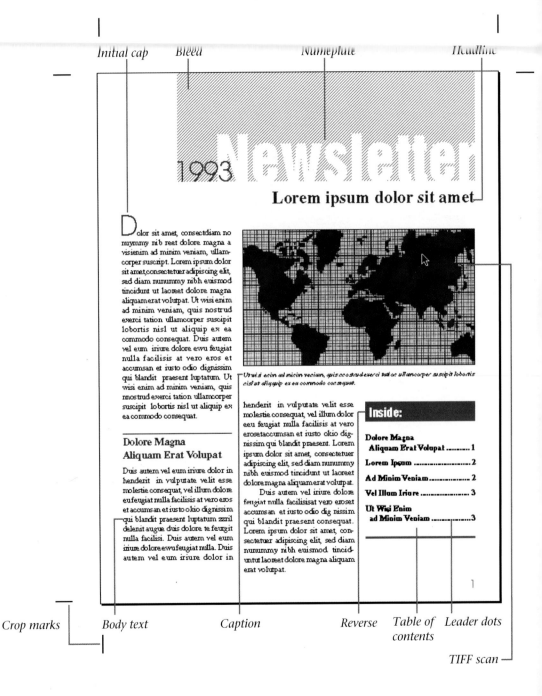

Initial cap   Bleed   Nameplate   Headline

1993 Newsletter

Lorem ipsum dolor sit amet

Dolor sit amet, consectdiam no nummy nib reet dolore magna a visienim ad minim veniam, ullamcorper suscipt. Lorem ipsum dolor sit amet,consectetuer adipiscing elit, sed diam nummmy nibh euismod tincidunt ut laoreet dolore magna aliquam erat volutpat. Ut wisi enim ad minim veniam, quis nostrud exerci tation ullamcorper suscipit lobortis nisl ut aliquip ex ea commodo consequat. Duis autem vel eum iriure dolore ewu feugiat nulla facilisis at vero eros et accumsan et iusto odio dignissim qui blandit praesent luptatum. Ut wisi enim ad minim veniam, quis mostrud exerci tation ullamcorper suscipit lobortis nisl ut aliquip ex ea commodo consequat.

Utwisi enim ad minim veniam, quis nostrud exerci tation ullamcorper suscipit lobortis eist ut aliquip ex ea commodo consequat.

Dolore Magna Aliquam Erat Volupat

Duis autem vel eum iriure dolor in henderit in vulputate velit esse molestie consequat, vel illum dolore eufeugiat nulla facilisis at vero eros et accumsan et iusto okio dignissim qui blandit praesent luptatum zzril delenit augue duis dolore te feurgit nulla facilisi. Duis autem vel eum iriure dolore ewufeugiat nulla. Duis autem vel eum iriure dolor in

henderit in vulputate velit esse molestie consequat, vel illum dolor eeu feugiat nulla facilisis at vero erosetaccumsan et iusto okio dignissim qui blandit praesent. Lorem ipsum dolor sit amet, consectetuer adipiscing elit, sed diam nummmy nibh euismod tincidunt ut laoreet dolore magna aliquamerat volutpat.

Duis autem vel iriure dolore feugiat nulla facilisisat vero eroset accumsan et iusto odio dig nissim qui blandit praesent consequat. Lorem ipsum dolor sit amet, consectetuer adipiscing elit, sed diam nummmy nibh euismod. tincid-untut laoreet dolore magna aliquam erat volutpat.

Inside:

Crop marks   Body text   Caption   Reverse   Table of contents   Leader dots

TIFF scan

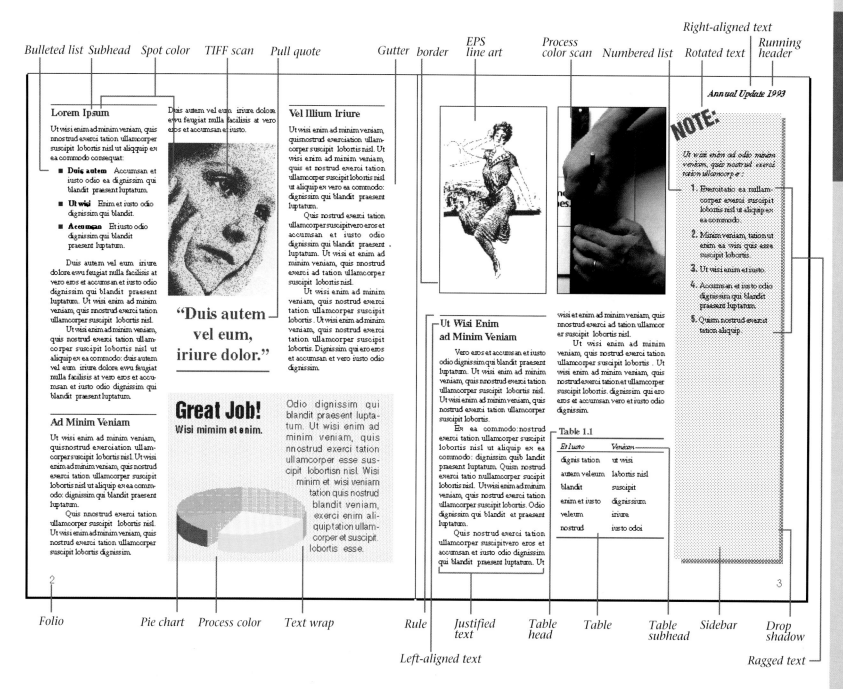

Bulleted list   Subhead   Spot color   TIFF scan   Pull quote   Gutter   border   EPS line art   Process color scan   Numbered list   Rotated text   Right-aligned text   Running header

Annual Update 1993

Lorem Ipsum

Ut wisi enim ad minim veniam, quis nnostrud exerci tation ullamcorper suscipit lobortis nisl ut aliquip ex ea commodo consequat:

- **Duis autem** Accumsan et iusto odio ea dignissim qui blandit praesent luptatum.
- **Ut wisi** Enim et iusto odio dignissim qui blandit.
- **Accumsan** Et iusto odio dignissim qui blandit praesent luptatum.

Duis autem vel eum iriure dolore ewu feugiat nulla facilisis at vero eros et accumsan et iusto odio dignissim qui blandit praesent luptatum. Ut wisi et enim ad minim veniam, quis nnostrud exerci tation ullamcorper suscipit lobortis nisl.

Ut wisi enim ad minim veniam, quis nostrud exerci tation ullamcorper suscipit lobortis nisl ut aliquip ex ea commodo: duis autem vel eum iriure dolore ewu feugiat nulla facilisis at vero eros et accumsan et iusto odio dignissim qui blandit praesent luptatum.

Ad Minim Veniam

Ut wisi enim ad minim veniam, quisnostrud exerciation ullamcorper suscipit lobortis nisl. Ut wisi enim ad minim veniam, quis nostrud exerci tation ullamcorper suscipit lobortis nisl ut aliquip ex ea commodo: dignissim qui blandit praesent luptatum.

Quis nnostrud exerci tation ullamcorper suscipit lobortis nisl. Ut wisi enim ad minim veniam, quis nostrud exerci tation ullamcorper suscipit lobortis dignissim.

Duis autem vel eum iriure dolore ewu feugiat nulla facilisis at vero eros et accumsan et iusto.

"Duis autem vel eum, iriure dolor."

Great Job!
Wisi mimim et enim.

Odio dignissim qui blandit praesent luptatum. Ut wisi enim ad minim veniam, quis nnostrud exerci tation ullamcorper esse suscipit lobortisn nisl. Wisi minim et wisi veniam tation quis nostrud blandit veniam, exerci enim aliquiptation ullamcorper et suscipit lobortis esse.

Vel Illium Iriure

Ut wisi enim ad minim veniam, quisnostrud exerciation ullamcorper suscipit lobortis nisl. Ut wisi enim ad minim veniam, quis et nostrud exerci tation ullamcorper suscipit lobortis nisl ut aliquip ex vero ea commodo: dignissim qui blandit praesent luptatum.

Quis nostrud exerci tation ullamcorper suscipitvero eros et accumsan et iusto odio dignissim qui blandit praesent luptatum. Ut wisi et enim ad minim veniam, quis nnostrud exerci ad tation ullamcorper suscipit lobortis nisl.

Ut wisi enim ad minim veniam, quis nnostrud exerci tation ullamcorper suscipit lobortis. Ut wisi enim ad minim veniam, quis nostrud exerci tation ullamcorper suscipit lobortis. Dignissim qui ero eros et accumsan et vero iusto odio dignissim.

Ut Wisi Enim ad Minim Veniam

Vero eros et accumsan et iusto odio dignissim qui blandit praesent luptatum. Ut wisi enim ad minim veniam, quis nnostrud exerci tation ullamcorper suscipit lobortis nisl. Ut wisi enim ad minim veniam, quis nostrud exerci tation ullamcorper suscipit lobortis.

Ex ea commodo: nostrud exerci tation ullamcorper suscipit lobortis nisl ut aliquip ex ea commodo: dignissim quib landit praesent luptatum. Quisn nostrud exerci tatio nullamcorper suscipit lobortis nisl. Ut wisi enim ad minim veniam, quis nostrud exerci tation ullamcorper suscipit lobortis. Odio dignissim qui blandit et praesent luptatum.

Quis nostrud exerci tation ullamcorper suscipitvero eros et accumsan et iusto odio dignissim qui blandit praesent luptatum. Ut

wisi et enim ad minim veniam, quis nnostrud exerci ad tation ullamcor er suscipit lobortis nisl.

Ut wisi enim ad minim veniam, quis nostrud exerci tation ullamcorper suscipit lobortis . Ut wisi enim ad minim veniam, quis nostrudexerci tation et ullamcorper suscipit lobortis. dignissim qui ero eros et accumsan vero et iusto odio dignissim

Table 1.1

Et Iusto	Veniam
dignis tation	ut wisi
autem vel eum	labortis nisl
blandit	suscipit
enim et iusto	dignissium
veleum	iriure
nostrud	iusto odoi

NOTE:

Ut wisi enim ad odio minim veniam, quis nostrud exerci tation ullamcorper:

1. Exercitatio ea nullamcorper exerci suscipit lobortis nisl ut aliquip ex ea commodo.
2. Minim veniam, tation ut enim ea wisi quis esse suscipit lobortis.
3. Ut wisi enim et iusto.
4. Accumsan et iusto odio dignissim qui blandit praesent luptatum.
5. Quism nostrud exerci tation aliquip.

Folio   Pie chart   Process color   Text wrap   Rule   Justified text   Table head   Table   Table subhead   Sidebar   Drop shadow

Left-aligned text

Ragged text

2

3

Good design requires more than just good taste. The successful designer will learn how to manipulate effects such as color, balance, rhythm, type selection, consistency, and graphics to create an effective and beautiful design without abusing the tremendous power of PageMaker. Often the most effective design can be achieved with simplicity.

This leather-bound illustrated history of England (over 200 years old), uses many of the design and typesetting conventions we use today. Columns, initial caps, rules, captions, and headlines were already in use by 1785.

Graphic design has become a common curriculum at colleges and universities only within the past 50 years. The ancient art of typography on the other hand dates back to the 13th century when bronze cast type was used in Korea. Half a century later, Johann Gutenberg awakened the West with his invention of moveable type, which led to the beginning of the Renaissance and Modern History.

The crafts of typesetting, design, and printing have developed a body of knowledge about what works and what does not. Electronic publishing has added to that knowledge, and has given many people the tools that were formerly available only to professionals.

What makes good design is always a subjective judgment. It is easier to identify the reasons why you don't like something than to identify why you do. Nevertheless, when you set out to design a page, think of the following design principles to help make your project a success.

A first rule of design:
Design for your reader, not yourself.
It is said that the best design is invisible. A good design gives precedence to the information contained in the document—without calling attention to itself. Your reader will appreciate your design if it does not get in the way of what is to be read.

There are three goals you should keep in mind regarding readers:

- Attract the reader
- Make your work easy to read
- Motivate the reader to do something

Some designers attract the reader with an unusual or beautiful layout, but fail at guiding the reader through with clarity and motivation. Unless you have a specific reason for making your reader work hard, (and there may be reasons why that would be desirable) make all design decisions guided by this rule.

Much is known about what makes reading easy. Generally, lines of text more than ten or twelve words long are difficult for the eye to track back and forth; as a result, designers utilize columns. Indents at the beginning of each paragraph create a visual cue that a new thought is being introduced. Certain typefaces are easier to comprehend in a paragraph, and others can make a headline catch the reader's eye. Also, there are several tricks for organizing and highlighting text that attract the eye and help organize information.

A second rule of design:
Listen to your client.
Your client is the reason you are designing. If the client is budget conscious, work accordingly. If the client likes red, don't insist on blue—unless you are convinced that it is better. Get all the information you can from the client. Ask questions such as:

- What is the budget?
- What is the time frame?
- Who is the audience?
- What do you want the reader to do?
- Who are your competitors?
- How have you reached your audience in the past?
- What is the existing corporate identity?

Find out what the client wants to achieve with the publication. Determine how to reach those goals. This does not mean that you should give in to every suggestion your client makes. The good designer offers general directional ideas, pointing out what can be achieved within time and budget constraints. More specific design ideas evolve as your project develops.

Electronic design with programs such as Aldus PageMaker offers the further option of direct participation by the client in design development. Some electronic designers are comfortable with clients working beside them at the computer. This can facilitate a very workable synthesis of ideas—or it can be disastrous. It also can dispel a client's perception that you just push a button and it is done—like magic! As a designer, you must establish comfortable boundaries.

A third rule of design:
Establish hierarchies and organize your information.

A hierarchy is a series of priorities for your design. Group articles into similar categories that use the same styles for heads and body copy. Choose appropriate sections of copy for sidebars or pull quotes. Some introductory text may benefit from a larger point size or different color. Determine where graphics will best support a topic or idea.

While you organize, be careful not to change the meaning of the copy provided to you. Paul Rand (designer of the famous IBM logo), decries the ease with which electronic publishing allows the emphasis of ideas in copy to be altered by a designer. The designer should never influence editorial content arbitrarily.

A fourth rule of design:
Establish a rhythm.

After you establish a hierarchy with the organization of headlines, subheads, body text, pull quotes, captions, and sidebars—you can begin to create a rhythm. In a typical book, rhythm can be established by the continuation of layout from one page to the next. This layout could include parallel columns of body copy, even or ragged-bottom margins, and the size and placement of graphics or photos—all important for developing page rhythm.

A tool that can help a designer establish rhythm is the thumbnail sketch—a small sketch of where basic elements on a page will go. Rhythm of a layout can be established quickly—in broad strokes and small size—using the thumbnail sketch. One difficulty of electronic page layout is that it discourages thumbnail sketching; the designer focuses on the specifics of the text, rather than the rhythm of the design. Keep the big picture in mind, as well as the details.

A fifth rule of design:
Pay attention to detail.

Nothing affects the quality of the design more than typographical errors or sloppy mistakes, such as rules that don't meet or uneven columns. It always is difficult to see your creation in an objective, fresh way; that is why it is a good idea to have someone else proofread for errors, consistency, and detail in your layout. Just as important is to take the time to run out final laser proofs before sending the file for final output—no matter how urgent the deadline. Skipping this crucial step invites disasters ranging from missed deadlines to a budget destroyed by the cost of extra imagesetting—or worse yet, a job that must be reprinted—at great cost to your client, or maybe yourself.

A sixth rule of design:
Work within your own limitations.

You cannot do more than the constraints of your time frame, budget, or abilities. As the designer, you interpret what is possible within the given parameters. Evaluate your strengths and weaknesses, and design according to your abilities. Illustrate, if you are a good illustrator. Don't attempt to create four-color process artwork if you don't understand how it works. You will be much more successful if you do what you do well, and call in experts when you need them. At the same time, work to expand your own abilities.

A seventh rule of design:
Design for your final output.
Output realities will influence electronic design decisions. For instance, if you plan to use a laser printer to run off 200 flyers, it would be foolish to scan graphics with a high resolution, because the printer can only print at 300 dots per inch. If you are imaging directly to film, you will not be able to physically paste in graphics that have not been converted to electronic format. If you are sending your publication by modem to a service bureau, you must build in the time it will take to send the files, especially if they include complex graphics.

An eighth rule of design:
Involve your printer up front.
The importance of this rule cannot be overstated. You should know who will print your work, the shop's capabilities, and have your questions answered even before you begin to design. The following list is only partial. Each project will involve specific additional questions:

- What are the financial terms?
- When will you need camera-ready art?
- Who is your contact person?
- Where can I save money by making design changes?
- What prepress tasks will be needed for this job? Who should do them?
- Do you prefer film or paper? Negatives or positives?
- What line-screen value should be used for halftones? (Assigned to scans used in PageMaker, varying for different printing processes.)
- What color matching systems do you support (PANTONE, Trumatch, and so forth)?
- Will I see a blueline? (Composite proof generated from film negatives.)
- Will I do a press check? (Checking the first few printed pieces before the full run is printed.)
- When will the work be finished?
- What is the rush charge policy?

Good printers are happy to answer these and other questions because they know that planning early pays off. Check through camera-ready art with your printer. It is time well spent. If a project is complex or large, the printer should be happy to talk to you about it before you begin working. You will find out much that can save you time and trouble later. For instance, many times, you achieve better quality if you let the printer make the halftones for photos and strip them into boxes you have left, rather than using scans. This is the kind of thing you may not know if you don't discuss your project with your commercial printer.

Designing with electronic tools, although based on the same concept, is not like using a pad of sketch paper and colored markers. The immediacy afforded by the computer means that design and production can begin simultaneously. There are tools and techniques that can emulate the experience of making traditional comps.

Thumbnails

Thumbnails are small sketches designers draw—often on tracing paper—before they place text and graphics into a document. They are a quick composite of an idea, giving the designer a sense of a document's layout, rather than focusing on the specifics.

To emulate the thumbnail sketching process in PageMaker, consider creating your initial design at 50% page view. It is also useful to print 50% reductions of your page designs to prevent focusing on details. You might also use the line tool to represent text, rather than actual words.

Printing thumbnails

Thumbnails in PageMaker are different from the traditional preliminary sketches by a designer. PageMaker thumbnails refer to printed reductions of several document pages on a single laser page. These can be very valuable when trying to make sense of a large, unwieldy document with many similar pages.

If you are not sure how many thumbnails you want on a printed page, try printing only a few pages of your document as thumbnails. This is because the processing time for printing can be long, and you may waste a lot of time only to find that you chose too few or too many thumbnails.

"Greek" text

Thank goodness for Lorem Ipsum—the text file that comes with PageMaker. It enables you to place columns of what's known as "greek" text—it is really Latin and semi-Latin—in your sample documents or templates.

Lorem Ipsum can be found under the unassuming name of "Text" in the Exploring directory in the tutorial file of PageMaker 5.0. Import it into your file by using the Place command under the File menu. It's so much easier than creating dummy text from scratch.

The main reason for using greek text is that clients can focus on a layout's aesthetics, rather than what it says. Another reason is that often copy is not yet ready for a document and the designer needs to use something as a placeholder. This is the situation where Lorem Ipsum is the perfect solution. Here are a number of considerations regarding Lorem Ipsum:

■ Lorem Ipsum is generally best for body text. You may want to use some typical sample headlines that a reader may find in the publication's final copy. You can go through earlier issues and choose some headlines for this purpose.

■ Be careful not to begin all the articles with the same sentence from Lorem Ipsum. This is especially true if you're showing how initial caps can be used; try several variations.

■ Pay attention to paragraph lengths when using Lorem Ipsum. Be sure they are irregular. You can do this by combining some paragraphs, and truncating others.

■ Lorem Ipsum does not hyphenate well, because PageMaker dictionaries do not include the words in their dictionaries. You can go through your text and type some hyphens arbitrarily to emulate hyphenation and right margins.

Mock-ups

Once you have created the initial design and layout for a document, it is time to make a mock-up. Create the mock-up so that you can solicit input and feedback from others—particularly from your client. It is important that the mock-up have the look and feel of the intended publication. Here are some suggestions for making laser-printed mock-ups:

- If you can, print sides of pages back-to-back by sending pages through the laser printer twice—once for the front and again for the back.

- If possible, use the paper stock that you will use for the publication. You may need to trim it to fit through your printer. You also may need to manually feed the paper if it is very thick.

- If you are printing a color publication, it is valuable to run your proofs on a color printer. Most service bureaus can provide color proofing, from 300 dot per inch laser prints to high resolution Matchprints. If your document is oversized, consider a Megachrome or Cactus print from a service bureau.

- If you are using bleeds in your final document, you may need to reduce the output size for your laser prints by selecting the Reduce to fit printing option. Crop marks then can be printed and the page trimmed to show the bleed.

- If you are creating a mock-up of a publication larger than 8 ½" x 11", print your pages as tiles, trim and tape the tiles together, leaving crop marks on the outside edges. Align the crop marks for the front and back of the page. Using a spray adhesive, attach the sides to each other and trim with a straight edge and matte knife.

Templates

PageMaker defines templates in two ways. One refers to a file that you create and save as a template. You then use the template as the basis for building future documents using the same type and layout specifications. Templates also can refer to the pre-designed publications supplied with PageMaker. We will look at both types:

- **Files saved as templates**

  By saving a file as a template, it can be used over and over to produce other documents with the same specifications. This is very useful when producing books—or any publication that uses repetitive elements. You create the initial design and save the document as a Template rather than a Publication. The next time you open this file, you will generate a copy rather than working on the original. Rename the new file when you save it for the first time. Your template remains unchanged.

▪ Pre-designed templates

Recognizing that not everyone is a designer, Aldus thoughtfully provides a number of templates for typical business documents (such as brochures, business cards, letterhead, labels, etc.). These predesigned templates work like the files you saved as templates: when opened, they create a file copy that you must rename when it is saved—leaving the original template unchanged.

These templates were designed with Times as the serif typeface and Helvetica as the sans serif typeface. You can change the typefaces by choosing Define styles (Control-3), and altering the specifications. If you change typefaces, you probably should keep the point sizes that are in the template, because they were designed to fit the measurements. After printing a proof or two, you can make adjustments to fit your particular publication.

The templates are found under Utilities, Aldus Additions, open template.

These are pages in the template called "Newsletter" under Aldus Additions.

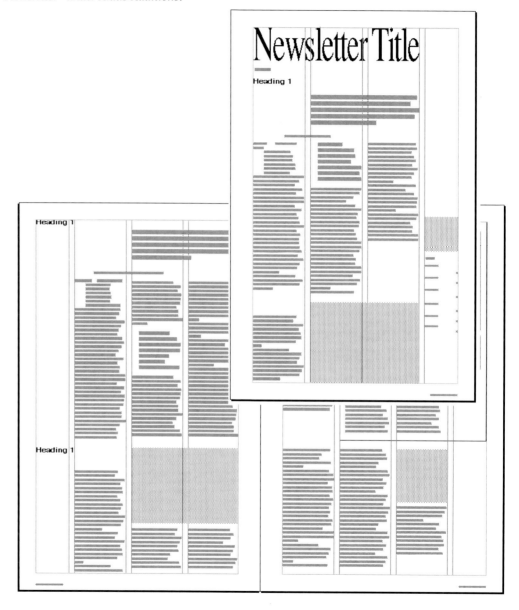

Document types

Different publications can require radically different planning and implementation strategies. This section discusses some basic design and technical considerations for some of the more common types of documents.

Advertisements

With ads, the challenge is to present the most valuable information into the largest space your client can afford. This may mean a full page, or it may mean a tiny one inch by one column format; you may have a budget for full color with page bleed, or you may be limited to black ink. In any case, think aggressively and effectively position your client's message relative to the other ads in the publication.

Design considerations:

- Look at a typical page where the ad you're creating will go. Decide what will make your ad stand out against other ads competing for attention on that page. Maybe the ad needs a strong border or a solid background. Often, simplicity in the midst of clutter will pull the reader's eye to your ad.

- When designing ads for telephone books and newspapers, avoid solid areas of black. Many publications use low grade paper where dot gain in printing may cause reverse type to fill in. Because of poor paper quality, also avoid subtle tonal differentiations and thin line art.

- Bleeds to the edge of the page can add impact to an ad. Usually bleeds are permissible only on full page ads.

- If the ad's main purpose is to motivate the reader to make a phone call, make sure the phone number is prominent. If the ad is meant to sell services requiring aesthetic judgment—such as haircutting or interior decoration—the ad should be in good taste and very stylish. When selling a particular product, a graphical depiction of the product is helpful.

- Small print is effective only after an ad has caught the reader's eye. Therefore the headline must be solid and strong. Very tight letterspacing or wordspacing, and minimal leading can help reinforce headlines that are read as one strong idea—and also save expensive ad space for your client.

- While white space is important in all designs, you should use it sparingly in ads, because of the cost of the "real estate."

Technical considerations:

- Get specifications for camera-ready artwork directly from the publication(s) before you begin your design. Most publications are willing to fax specifications to a designer—or do almost anything else—to make it easy to run ads.

- Because deadlines are critical, verify your due date, the mailing address, and the contact person with the publication.

- Publications are picky about what line screen they will accept. Generally, if the ad is for a newspaper, you don't want a line screen above 90; if it's for a medium-quality magazine, 110 to 120 is a safe bet. Higher-end publications can accept 133 to 175 line screen. (See Line screens, page 147.)

- Many publications will not accept paste-up ads, but require that you submit a photostat. If you have composed all the elements of your ad on the computer screen, you can simply send high resolution PostScript output (such as Linotronic paper or film). Some publications accept files on disk.

- If you are creating a four-color ad, determine whether the publication accepts separated film output. In some cases, they prefer to do the color separation for you, in which case you simply provide color photographs leaving boxes for their placement in the film artwork. You also will need to provide a laser print with a low-resolution grayscale scan of the photograph sized and cropped FPO (for position only).

Annual reports

The purpose of an annual report is to show the organization publishing the report in its best light to shareholders or others who have an interest in that organization.

Often, the format is an 8 ¹/₂" x 11" booklet. Because of the "image" nature of the document, good design is essential. Most large corporations retain famous designers for their annual reports, and a lot of the work is in a rather conventional vein. There are those, however, that take chances—like the one shown here.

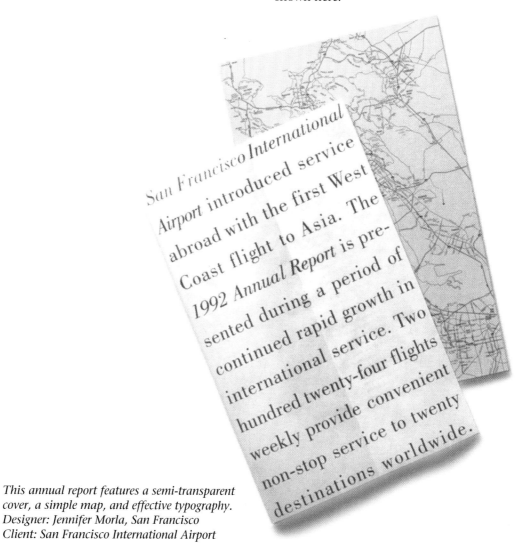

This annual report features a semi-transparent cover, a simple map, and effective typography.
Designer: Jennifer Morla, San Francisco
Client: San Francisco International Airport

Document types

Books

PageMaker is excellent for creating books. Its indexing and table of contents capabilities, and the way it can link chapters together from multiple publications, make PageMaker a natural for book publishing.

Creating a sample chapter is the simplest way to create a book in PageMaker. Once you have created this chapter and saved it as a template, you can flow word-processed text into it and save each chapter with a new name.

Design considerations:

■ There are standard trim sizes for books. Designing within these configurations will reduce your printing costs, as well as make the book more "stockable" at bookstores.

■ Any book of significant thickness should have a larger margin (or gutter) between left and right pages to allow for binding.

■ Design appropriately for the subject. An instructional book, such as this one, should accommodate multiple graphics and make use of full-color printing; a textbook, particularly for higher grade levels, can be designed for one- or two-color printing. A novel or biography is usually printed in one color.

■ Books need a rigid hierarchy that the reader can grasp immediately. Chapter openers, running headers, title pages, parts pages, and headline sizes—should be consistent and dependable.

■ A serif typeface is recommended for copy that you place in a book—if it has any length at all. To use a sans serif would be too much work for the reader.

■ Design books to accommodate reflow. This is what happens when the author or editor makes changes to the text that will result in elements overflowing to a new page. That means various elements should work equally well on a verso (left) as well as on a recto (right) page.

Technical considerations:

■ Books require page numbers. PageMaker has automatic page numbering as part of its master pages feature.

■ Use of paragraph style definitions are a given in book layout; without them you may be hard pressed to achieve consistency.

■ Master pages are very important for books. Know how to set up a master page and also how to override master-page elements.

It is easy to link separate chapter publications together to facilitate printing, automate page numbering, indexing, and table of contents of the book. Here is how it's done:

1. In any chapter publication, choose Book from under the File menu.

2. Select each file that you want to include in the book.

3. Decide whether to have auto renumbering across publications take place. If so, you may want to have each new file begin on an odd- or even-numbered page.

4. To copy the new book list into all the other files in the list, hold down the Control key and choose Book again; a dialog box will tell you that it is copying the book list.

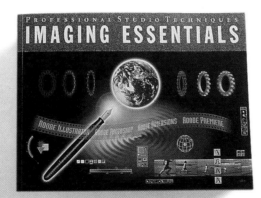

This book exhibits a very contemporary cover design with color and simplicity.
Designer: Eric Baker
Client: Adobe Press

Brochures

Brochures extend an organization's corporate identity. They can illuminate the organization's goals, or what it sells. Brochures are one of the designer's best opportunities to extend boundaries and be creative because there is often a larger budget for brochures than for other elements comprising the corporate identity.

Design considerations:

■ Brochures should be easy to keep around and should fit into letter-sized file folders.

■ Unless you are trying to project an upscale image of the product or organization, brochures should not appear expensive.

■ Brochures need to be very stylish and can benefit from devices such as initial caps, sidebars, and pull quotes.

■ Brochures should always follow the client's corporate identity program. Because brochures often are presented with an accompanying letter, proposal, or business card, use of logos should be consistent in color, placement, and so forth. Sometimes it is necessary to use a certain typeface in order to reinforce the identity.

■ Brochures should be rich in graphics. Graphs and charts, pictures of products and people, or sometimes just a graphical theme should be carried throughout the piece. Brochures must be more than text.

■ Three-fold brochures are an inexpensive and efficient solution. They are made by folding a printed sheet twice. 8 ½" x 11", 8½" x 14", and 11" x 17" pages all can be folded to make excellent 3-fold brochures.

■ Brochures must always include a phone number and a call to action, such as "Call us today for a free estimate."

Technical considerations:

■ Color is used more frequently in brochures than in many other PageMaker projects.

■ Bleeds are often possible without extra cost because brochures are usually trimmed.

■ Multiple pages often are part of a brochure—so when creating a PageMaker file for a brochure, it's useful to use Master Pages.

■ Brochures often are printed in great quantities. This means that high-quality printing, using metal plates rather than paper ones, is usually more appropriate.

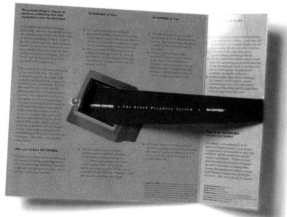

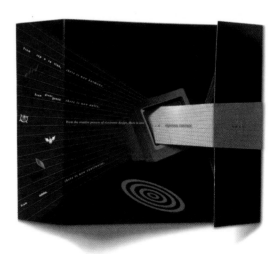

Both sides of this brochure take advantage of three-dimensionality using exciting graphics and color.
Designer: Cindy Chin, Studio MD, Seattle
Client: Printing Control

Calendars

Calendars make great holiday gifts for organizations to give clients. Because they are useful, a company can have advertising in front of its clients throughout the entire year. Each page can carry a new message reinforcing the perception the company wants to create.

It is imperative that calendars be beautiful as well as useful. PageMaker is an ideal program for producing calendars.

Design considerations:

■ Calendars should be held together with a common theme. They usually require several pieces of art.

■ The more useful the calendar, the more likely it will be kept; therefore, design calendars that have room on which to write.

■ Clutter in a calendar is very distracting. Simplicity is more important here than in many other types of documents. Try to keep advertising messages to a minimum.

■ Calendars usually follow a standard layout with the weeks in a horizontal format, and with the days of the week beginning with Sunday.

Technical considerations:

■ Experiment with the benefits of one large text block for the dates versus small, threaded text blocks. This is important when updating the different months in the calendar.

■ Tabs and indents are useful when setting up the number grids.

■ Consider using the master pages for the graphical elements of the calendar grid.

■ Kerning numerals closer together is important, especially when the 1 is part of the number.

This calendar uses a traditional format, and makes innovative use of a keyboard motif for the days of the month.
Designers: Debbie Torgan & Maureen Kane
Client: PRINTZ Electronic Design, San Francisco

Catalogs

PageMaker is the perfect program for producing catalogs. Its capability to import word-processing style definitions means that numerous kinds of text treatments for headlines, product names, descriptions, prices, and stock numbers can be applied throughout the document. Order forms can take advantage of tabs and leader.

Design considerations:

■ Establish a grid and stick to it throughout the publication. Readers of catalogs adapt quickly to a page layout and expect it to remain consistent page after page.

■ Typestyles should remain consistent. Headlines, names of items, descriptions of items, model numbers, and prices should stay in the same typefaces from page to page. Very little can be gained from variation for its own sake.

■ Copy should be kept as small as possible, with photographs or drawings of the products featured prominently. (This rule is not always ironclad. For instance, a scientific brochure where the products all look similar, but vary primarily in their specifications, would require larger type and smaller pictures.)

■ Forms are a necessary part of a catalog and should be simple to understand and fill out. (See Coupons, page 98.)

■ You often see Initial Caps used in catalogs. (See Initial Caps, page 92.)

Technical considerations:

■ Paragraph style definitions are indispensable when creating a catalog.

■ Text Wrap also works well with catalogs. (See page 130 for more information on Text Wrap.)

■ Scans are excellent in catalogs, and are easy to organize in a program such as Aldus Fetch. You can store them on different disks and drives, and have a ready reference when placing them.

■ Photo CD is an efficient way to store a large number of scans, but can be cumbersome when it is time to place them.

■ Bleeds can be used as reference tabs and are often used in catalogs. (See Bleeds, page 58.)

The design elements of this catalog are numerous. It combines rhythm, color, balance, with unexpected surprises.
Design by: Pentagram Design, San Francisco
Client: The Nature Company

Document types

Corporate identity

Logos, letterhead, envelopes, labels, business cards, and signs all contribute to an organization's corporate identity.

Designing a corporate identity—whether for the corner store or a major company—should be approached only after you have gathered as much information about the organization as possible. You should know your client's products, services, market, competition, sales plan, and goals. Once established, a corporate identity should be inviolable. Recommend that the organization create a style manual that sets out the uses of the organization's logo, colors, address lines, and so forth.

Design considerations:

- Design the logo first.

- Make the logo effective in its simplest format. In other words, assume that it will sometimes appear in all black and white. Does it look good that way, or does it require colors to work?

- Make the logo effective when used at any size. Would it look as good atop a tall skyscraper as it does in a tiny newspaper ad?

- Make the logo in equal proportions in height and width. Sometimes it will appear in a narrow space, and if it is too horizontal it will need to appear very small in order to keep its proportions.

- Go for simplicity and timelessness. Use classic rather than trendy typestyles. Make a logo that will last for years; assume that the organization will never want to change it.

- Choose colors that always can be matched. Consider PANTONE or other color matching systems.

- Determine that the paper you choose is a stocked item before specifying it.

Technical considerations:

- Create logo and logo-type artwork files outside PageMaker, if possible, so that they can be imported and sized as a unit.

- Place artwork for envelopes, labels, and sometimes even letterhead on the same tabloid size page rather than several smaller pages to cut down on image-setting costs.

Letterhead and envelopes

Letterhead usually conveys a restrained organization or company image. After all, letters are as likely to contain bad news as they are good. Letterhead should be businesslike and unemotional.

Letterhead can be beautiful too. Again, design with the reader in mind. Only this time, imagine the invisible part—the body of the typical letter—and ensure that the message is the easiest part of the letter to read.

Design considerations:

- Print letterhead, envelopes, and business cards at the same time thereby minimizing the set-up charge for additional colors.

- Downplay logo, address, and phone number, because most important is the information contained in the letter. (Don't go overboard—make sure these elements are all legible.)

- Specify typical letter layouts so your client is aware of how information can complement your design.

- Choose paper that is readily available for those times when the client realizes he/she is out of letterhead two days before a planned 10,000-piece mailing.

- Before choosing a paper stock, make sure there are matching envelopes, even if you are not printing the envelopes.

Technical considerations:

- 8 ¹/₂" x 11" format is standard.

- Check the job when it is at the printer, because most clients are more particular about their letterhead and envelopes than other publications.

- Keep careful records of color and paper choices, because clients will always call you for them.

This corporate identity combines the low cost of two-color printing with a modern look. It uses a bleed, a custom designed font, and unusual colors.
Designer: Michael J. Nolan
Client: CDRT, San Francisco

Business cards

Business cards grease the wheels of commerce and have become a cultural ritual in American society. Have you ever met with someone and wanted to send a thank you letter afterwards, but didn't know how to spell the last name? The business card provides instant access, by mail or phone, to the person and his or her company or organization.

Design considerations:

- Business cards are 2" x 3.5". You will see oversized or undersized cards, but they are unwise because many people file cards in holders or books and the nonconforming card doesn't get filed.

- Use both sides of a business card to convey information. The back side of a card can contain graphics or other "secondary" information.

This design takes advantage of both sides of the business card. The glossy stock and dash of unexpected color draw attention to the company's primary services.
Designer: Michael J. Nolan
Client: Suzanne Clark Productions, San Francisco

- Phone numbers should be prominent and should include area codes. Complete addresses with postal codes are also necessary.

- Design for the longest name imaginable in the allocated name space, and for the longest title in the allocated title space.

- The business card must conform to the corporate identity in every way possible: ink color, paper choice, typestyle, logotype, and so forth.

Technical considerations:

- The Power Paste feature is useful in laying out business cards.

- Business cards can be laid out 10 up on an 8 ½" x 11" page.

Disk labels

Disk labels for CDs, floppy disks, video, or audio cassettes are often an afterthought, but should be treated as part of a corporate identity program. PageMaker is useful because disk labels can require type to be set upside down or sideways, and precise measurements are possible.

Design considerations:

- Type must be very small. Choose a very readable face and stay away from reverses if possible.

- Pay attention to white space. A label with little or no margin is uninviting.

- Leave plenty of room for the title of the work and the name of the artist.

Technical considerations:

- Because type is so small, high-resolution imagesetting is almost always necessary.

- Lay out as many labels as will fit on an 8 ½" x 11" page. You can print them on self-adhesive paper that comes in many grades and colors.

- Bleeds can be set up at little or no additional cost on disk labels or cassette covers, since labels must usually be trimmed.

- Labels for CDs are printed on the disk itself. You can use one to four colors, and preparing the artwork is actually quite simple.

Flyers

Whether for a school play or a neighborhood store super sale, flyers can convey valuable information. Flyers were one of the first document types that desktop publishing impacted. Today they present some of the best and worst designs the technology affords.

It must be that designers think of flyers as the ultimate throwaway. They are usually given little design consideration: often quick-printed on gaudy-colored paper. You find them stuck under your windshield wiper and you go to throw them away—until, what's this, an interesting design? Read on...

Design considerations:

■ Although there are few limitations on how much can be printed on a flyer, it is still important to present information in hier-archical fashion, broken into digestible chunks.

■ If the flyer is a handout, rather than posted on a bulletin board, consider using both sides of the paper for extra information.

■ Consider a color of ink other than black.

■ Grab attention with one strong headline.

■ For posted flyers, include a row of tear-off telephone numbers or other reminders.

■ Dark colored paper makes flyers harder to read. Use good graphics to make flyers eye-catching.

Technical considerations:

■ Flyers can be printed in limited quantities on laser printers.

■ Because flyers are usually printed on stan-dard size paper, they cannot incorporate bleeds unless they are trimmed to a smaller size.

■ For flyers photocopied from high-resolution imagesetter positives, use a line screen value of 85 or 90 for graphics.

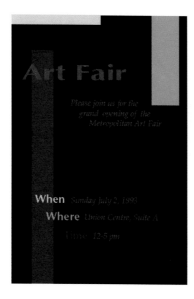

Invitations

Designers usually find invitations a pleasant assignment. The goal is to set a mood for an event and entice the recipient to attend. Invitations can be very traditional, as in the case of a wedding; or offbeat, as may be the case for a theatrical fundraiser. Of course, nothing is wrong with an offbeat wedding invitation.

Design considerations:

■ Use a standard size invitation because it will fit a standard size envelope.

■ Use an 80# text stock or heavier.

■ Bleeds are easy to effect because most invitations require trimming.

■ Answer the basic "who, what, when, where, why, how much, and what do I have to do to get tickets?" questions.

■ You may need to include a return card and an envelope for it.

■ A map may be necessary. Consider a drawing program like Aldus FreeHand or Intellidraw.

Technical considerations:

■ Invitations can often be printed two-up on an 8 1/2" x 11" or 8 1/2" x 14" sheet.

■ Crop and fold marks are important be-cause most invitations must be trimmed and folded.

Menus

What a feast for the designer! You have a very special assignment when you are asked to create a menu. Your task is to make the restaurant's dishes look wholesome and delicious—worth ordering. Visualize the restaurant as somewhere you may find yourself some Saturday night. Your job is to make the restaurant appear great.

Design considerations:

■ Menus should give the impression of abundance and wide choice.

■ Organize with different categories in mind: appetizers, salads, soups, main courses, desserts, and so forth.

■ As a rule, friendly warm fonts work best with food. Use cold, modern fonts only for austere upscale places that serve undercooked vegetables in small portions.

■ Three-fold menus work especially well.

■ Graphics are very important, as is color printing. Ethnic foods lend themselves to thematic graphic interpretations, but try to avoid the cliches.

■ If the establishment has a logo, always use it. If not, create one and use it.

■ There is a wealth of clip art for menu use.

■ A menu that is too slick or overproduced suggests a chain restaurant.

Technical considerations:

■ Menus must be durable if used day after day. Print on a heavy stock and consider lamination.

■ Make it simple to change the prices.

Newsletters

If you design a newsletter that is so successful it has a 2nd, 3rd, 4th, or 10th edition, congratulate yourself. Not only have you designed a powerful piece, but you have made it so easy to produce that clients just keep coming back for more!

Successful newsletter design and production must be based on efficiency. Deadlines are central to the process. No one respects a quarterly newsletter that comes out twice a year. Unless a last-minute submission is time-sensitive, save it for the next issue.

Design considerations:

■ Generally, a newsletter should not look like it was expensive to produce. In fact, designing for inexpensive printing ensures that you will have the opportunity to design the piece more frequently.

■ A friendly, informal (but professional) tone should be taken in newsletters.

■ Newsletters can be many different sizes other than the common 11" x 17" folded to 8 1/2" x 11". For variation, try a 17" x 22" folded once to tabloid size, or 11" x 17" folded twice into a three-fold format.

■ Self-mailer newsletters are the most environmentally responsible.

■ Newsletters should be consistent from issue to issue. Use the same paper, layout, fonts, column headings, and nameplate.

Technical considerations:

■ Often, many people do the data entry for stories. This means you must depend on spell-checking and search and replace features found in PageMaker's story editor to clean up text.

■ Photographs can be supplied by every district office and sales manager in the company. They will be inconsistent in appearance and quality, so take care in scanning and cropping photographs.

This newsletter shows an excellent balance of informality with a professional look.
Designer: The NewsLetter Company, Campbell, CA
Client: San Jose Medical Group

Newspapers

When designing a newspaper, you should take pride in knowing it will be an important source of information for many people. While you want readers to notice that the paper looks good, you don't want them to be overly aware of the design. Again, the information is the most important consideration.

More newspapers today are using four-color printing as they compete with television and other media for the buyer's attention. This poses more challenges for the newspaper designer, but also affords more opportunity.

Design considerations:

■ The reader is looking for a concise organization of information in a newspaper.

■ Sections should be clearly identified, as should recurring columns and other features.

■ A newspaper needs to look like a newspaper. Find the ones you like the best and see what works for them.

■ Page size is usually limited. Certain formats work with readers and those are what readers prefer.

■ To make it easy for potential advertisers to prepare camera-ready art for ads, use easy-to-measure standard column sizes.

■ Paragraph styles in PageMaker must be tightly defined and controlled, or the paper can quickly lose its identity. Desktop publishing means that many people will have a hand in the creation and output of the final pages.

■ Justified text is almost a given for a newspaper to look like a newspaper.

Technical considerations:

■ Oversize pages necessitate high-resolution imagesetting, or tiled laser prints.

■ Ads may require physical paste up, coming from numerous sources.

■ Low quality newsprint dictates line screens of 85-90 for graphics.

Posters

Posters are probably the closest publication to fine art. Perhaps that is why you find so many framed and on walls. They are a unique and personal way of advertising.

Design considerations:

- Large format requires thinking big. Make graphics and type as large as possible.

- Color creates impact in posters. If you don't have a big budget for printing, use colored paper and one or two ink colors.

- When you think about designing a poster, think drama.

Technical considerations:

- Since posters often are collected and displayed long after the event they advertise, use good quality paper for printing them.

- If you start with original art that is very small and use it for scanned graphics in the poster, flaws will be exaggerated.

The poster shown here relies on bold graphics and a striking positive/negative interplay to capture attention.
Designer: Jennifer Morla, San Francisco
Client: Capp Street Project

Programs

Programs for events often change at the last minute. Whether for small community groups or expositions, a program must communicate immediacy. It is a snapshot in time: this event, this date. Programs always invite the designer to experiment, be playful and break the boundaries.

Design considerations:

■ Most theatrical and other groups need to keep costs down, and therefore programs should be straightforward and efficient to print.

■ Because most programs include ads, the page layout must accommodate them.

■ Photos of actors or other participants add interest and life to a program.

■ Programs follow fairly rigid formats, from their (typical) 5 ¹/₂" x 8 ¹/₂" size, to their progression of information.

■ Graphics are essential for program covers, and also liven up interiors.

The video exposition program below shows many of the elements found in programs, such as schedules and registration information. Created within a small budget, it uses two colors: a metallic and black ink.
Designer: Michael J. Nolan
Client: Knowledge Industries, Inc.

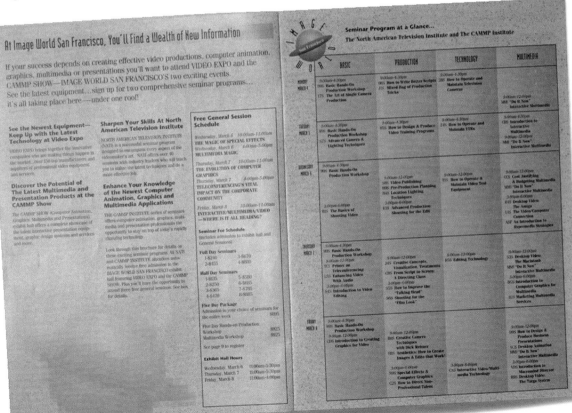

Résumés

The desktop production of résumés has changed the way people look for jobs. Savvy job hunters now know that nothing less than a typeset, laser-printed résumé on quality paper stock will do.

Of course, the design of a résumé depends on the kind of job sought. An accountant should have a very different looking résumé from that of an actor. If there is any doubt about which way to go, the rule is simple: straightforward and free from adornment.

Design considerations:

■ The average résumé is given about 15 seconds consideration by its recipient. Design accordingly.

■ Use more than one column to "beef up" paragraphs. One or two lines of text across an entire page will take up three or four lines on a half-page column. This makes the applicant's accomplishments look meatier.

■ Create an aura of class, accomplishment, and sophistication for your client.

■ Use bullet points wherever possible.

■ Avoid abbreviations for states, titles, and other categories.

When a résumé is arranged in two columns, job descriptions and achievements fill additional lines, making them look more substantial.

Technical considerations:

■ Most clients want adaptability for changing job objectives, and easy updating of a résumé. Make it easy to change.

■ Most résumés will be laser printed. Choose a paper stock that looks good with laser-quality type, and avoid graphics that require high resolution to look good.

EILEEN A. FRANKLIN

1142 Halsted Street
Chicago, Illinois 60625
312-864-3757 (home)
312-425-2314 (work)

Education

• Masters Health Services Administration
College of Saint Francis
Joliet, Illinois
May 1992

School of Public and Environmental Affairs
University of Illinois
Champaign, Illinois
21 Graduate hours completed in Public Administration 1979-1982

• BS Nursing
University of Illinois
May 1974

Career Summary

SB HEALTHCARE
ST. BRIDGET'S HOSPITAL
Chicago, Illinois   2/89 - Present

Vice-President, Utilization/Quality Management

Director, Utilization Management,
Quality Assurance and Provider Relations

Responsibilities include the development and implementation of strategies to achieve cost effective, quality health service delivery for SB Healthcare members.

Achievements:
• Implemented a utilization management program focused on a cooperative approach with physicians. This program change supported a 34% reduction in bed days/1000 for the SBH members.
• Assisted with the formalization of a Physician Hospital Organization (PHO) for mental health/substance abuse services. This arrangement decreased inpatient mental health utilization by 70% for SBH members.
• Developed a dedicated program for the Medicare risk members to meet regulatory requirements and provide continuity of care for improved cost control and quality assurance.
• Participated in the budget process for SB Healthcare; identified organizational changes necessary to achieve staffing efficiencies with improved productivity.
• Participated on the SB Quality Council. This council directed all Total Quality management activities.
• Assisted with the identification and education of physician advisors who accepted responsibility for the control of cost-effective, quality focused health service delivery to SB Healthcare members.
• Chaired a Utilization Management Committee at St. Bridget's Hospital, which evaluated and recommended strategies for utilization control and improvements.
• Identified and developed a team of RNs who have maintained the SB Health commercial inpatient util-ization statistic at 294 bed days/1000.
• Negotiated contracts with physicians and other vendors to acquire competitive pricing and quality services.

HEALTH FIRST HMO
Bloomington, Illinois   1985 - 2/89

Vice-President, Medical Delivery Services

Implemented strategies to achieve inpatient utilization targets. Reorganized the Medical Delivery department to decrease personnel costs while achieving improved inpatient statistical outcomes. Developed informational reports used to discuss statistical outcomes with physicians, as well as identify areas requiring problem resolution. Negotiated hospital, physician and general vendor contracts for cost control and quality services. This position reported to the Chief Executive Officer.

Central Region Medical Manager

Acquired this position as the first staff person assigned to these responsibilities. Duties included hospital contract negotiation, physician contract negotiation and ancillary provider contract negotiation. Developed tracking methodologies to monitor health services delivery and associated costs. Managed provider relations and crisis resolution.

Early Career

Graduated from University of Illinois School of Nursing and began as a staff nurse delivering acute clinical services to the pediatric population at Champaign Children's Hospital. Worked with the County Health Department in supervisory and management positions. Developed and implemented the County Childhood Lead Poisoning Screening and Prevention Program which continues to function 8 years later. Created injury surveillance techniques for the County Injury Control Program. As a Project Nurse for the YWCA, developed the health program for a national project providing educational experiences for indigent mothers lacking formal education.

There are certain elements that many publications have in common—financial tables, nameplates, mastheads, sidebars—and the style in which these elements is treated must be consistent with the purpose and appearance of the document of which they are a part.

Covers

Books, magazines, and annual reports always have covers. Brochures, even if they are constructed from a three-fold sheet, have a section that serves as a cover; other documents have no cover. Covers fall into two categories: those that sell, and those that protect. Some covers do both.

Covers that sell

Books and magazines usually depend on their packaging to sell. They must observe some or all of the following conventions:

■ Covers usually contain numerous elements: title, subtitle, author, bullet copy, volume numbers, dates, illustrations, and so forth. It is crucial that these elements relate to one another. Creating a grid will make this much easier.

■ Place the title near the top, in a strong typeface.

■ Make sure that the color of any text appearing on the cover contrasts with the illustration behind it, so that it can be read easily.

■ If there is subsidiary information—such as a subtitle or text describing topics covered inside—it should be strongly styled.

■ Text on a multi-colored background may make uniform contrast difficult. Consider a drop shadow behind the text to make it stand out against the different shades.

■ Spend more resources (design time and printing budget) on the cover than the interior. This should yield a greater number of readers for the publication. It is not uncommon for publications with a one-color interior to have four-color covers.

■ Strive for unity between the cover and the interior. This can be achieved by using the same typefaces and colors, or by displaying illustrations or photos from the inside of the publication on the cover.

■ The spine of a book is considered as important as its front cover—because books are often displayed spine-out in stores. The only way to capture the buyer's eye is often with a thin strip of effective color and typography.

Covers that protect

Protecting the interior pages is another function of covers, particularly if the publication is being mailed. That's why the trade name for heavy paper is "cover stock." Here are some considerations about printing on heavy stock:

■ Folding heavy stock requires scoring so that the paper does not "break" along the fold.

■ Most paper stock that may be used for the interior pages of a document can be matched in a cover stock (80# or more). If you are using, for instance, a recycled, speckletone ivory stock for interior pages, either match it exactly in cover stock, or use a contrasting color in the same stock.

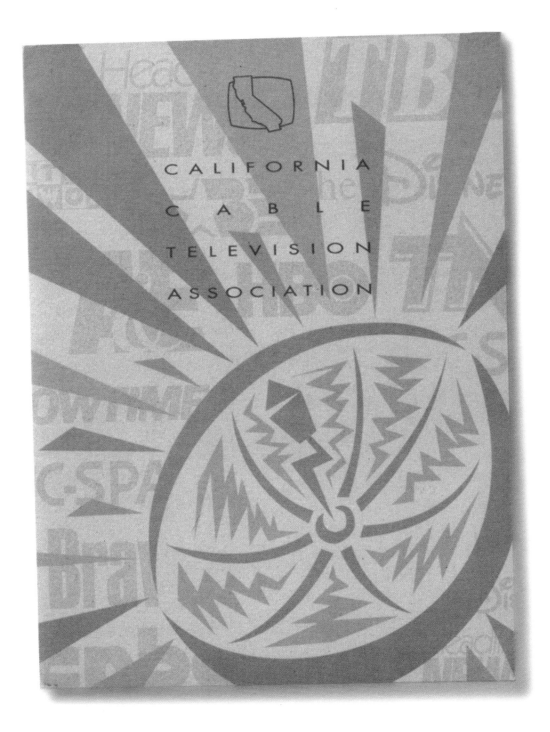

CALIFORNIA CABLE TELEVISION ASSOCIATION

Mastheads

Mastheads—found in newsletters, magazines and similar publications—are usually narrow columns near the table of contents page containing information such as editors' and publishers' names, the organization's name and address, volume and issue numbers, and so forth. Their characteristics are as follows:

■ Small type is usually used in mastheads. If you are using larger than eight point type, it is probably too large.

■ Mastheads should not be more than a column wide, and seldom more than half a page in height.

■ Mastheads can be set off by rules around them. They should not be a major graphical element, and usually do not call attention to themselves.

The cover to the left is a folder used to contain a brochure and data sheets. It is printed two-color on an 80# buff colored paper.
Designer: Mike Bertoni, PRINTZ Electronic Design, San Francisco.
Client: California Cable Television Association

Nameplates

A Nameplate which is the identifying title of a newsletter or magazine, is one of the most important design elements in a publication because it gives the reader a visual cue about what the document is.

Because the nameplate is the primary identification for your publication, it must convey the proper "attitude." Depending on the purpose of the document, it should be dignified, humorous, corporate, avant garde, child-like, old-fashioned, contemporary, reassuring, or upsetting. Here are some guidelines for designing nameplates:

■ Spend time designing the nameplate because it will be used with each issue and, once established, should not change.

■ Use strong typography and pay careful attention to hierarchy. The name of the publication is more important than the volume or issue number.

■ Make the name of the publication as large as possible; you can even increase the size of the text by few points after kerning the letters very tightly together. Downplay small words such as "The."

■ If possible, create the nameplate in a graphics program such as Aldus FreeHand or Adobe Illustrator. This enables you to import it into PageMaker as one object so that you can copy and reduce it for other pages.

■ Taglines such as "A Quarterly Newsletter from Organization X" are important to help the reader identify what is being presented.

■ If you want a lot of color in a publication, use color in the nameplate, and print enough shells (preprinted blank pages for all the issues you intend to publish) for the next year. This way, you can print the text and graphics for the succeeding issues in one or two colors, and only incur the setup charges for the nameplate colors one time. The disadvantage is that your printer has to store the shells, and your client has to pay for all the paper up front. An advantage is that it commits your client to future issues.

■ Make sure you relate the nameplate to the column format that appears below it —even if it spans all the columns. If you have a three-column format, perhaps one part of the nameplate spans one column, and another part is two columns wide.

■ If you are going to use the name of the month(s) to identify issues, design with "September/October" to determine the maximum amount of space you will need for future months.

■ Type placed vertically makes interesting nameplates.

Sidebars

Sidebars, which are related information set aside from other text with a special font or graphic treatment, serve as another "point of entry" into an article or page. Many times they are complete "stories" unto themselves, giving the reader a synopsis of the information that may be the only text read. Often, sidebars contain graphs, charts, or other visual information besides text. Sometimes, an entire article can be treated as a sidebar. Discovering a well-designed sidebar on a page gives the reader a feeling of sharing "a secret" by being privy to special information.

■ If a sidebar is primarily text, it is usually effective from a design standpoint to put it in a different font, or to use a different color for the type. This treatment is less common than the simple screened box which is often used.

■ A sidebar bleeding off the edge of page can be very effective, particularly if you use a gradient screen created in a program such as Aldus Freehand or Adobe Illustrator and import it.

■ If a sidebar fills a normal column, the text or graphics inside it should be narrower than that in columns, so that they have margins within the sidebar.

■ Sidebars are a good way to set up a table of contents on the front page of a newsletter. Use a heading such as "In this Issue" in a stylish type treatment.

Table of contents

Building a table of contents (TOC) for a book at one time was a laborious process—with great potential for accidentally listing a wrong page number if pages were changed. PageMaker has solved that problem, making it possible to create a table of contents for one or even several different files at once. Here is how it is done:

1. Decide whether to create a separate publication for a table of contents, or if it will go on a page of your current document. If you choose to have a separate publication, you will need to generate a book list. (See page 14.) Do not confuse generating a book list with the Aldus Addition Build booklet....

2. Determine which headings, (chapter names, subheads, and so forth), you are going to list in your table of contents.

3. PageMaker's table of contents is based upon a paragraph attribute setting. You can easily apply this attribute to styles.

4. Select Define styles (Control-3), from the Type menu, and double-click on a style for the paragraph you want to include in the table of contents.

5. Click on Para... and when the next dialog box opens, check Include in table of contents, found on the bottom line.

6. Repeat steps 4 and 5 for other styles that should be included in the TOC.

7. Close the Define styles dialog box.

8. Choose Create TOC from the Utilities menu, and select the settings you want; click on the OK button.

9. A loaded text icon will appear, that you then can place as any other text icon.

10. Format the table of contents with the correct type, indent, and tabbing specifications. Style definitions are automatically generated for tables of contents. It is best to change text formatting by changing those style definitions.

Tables

Tables can be challenging because they require extensive use of tabs, small point sizes, rules, reverses, headings, and other difficult elements. Tables often don't fit into columns; and are hard to make look good.

Tables are an important part of many publications, and can be simple and elegant. Once again, PageMaker contains the kind of powerful features that can make tables easy.

■ Designing tables

Whether for a service schedule, such as the one shown here, or for a financial report, information must be easy for the reader to find quickly. If there are numerous rows and columns, try differentiating them visually. You can use screens or rules to do this.

Lay out the text in your table before attempting to create screened backgrounds or rules to divide the columns. Use the longest word or number to determine the width of columns, and if you can, make the column widths equal. If they are, you will be able to use the Multiple paste feature to space them equally across the page.

Table headings should look different than the rest of the information. Try reverse text in a solid bar, or an italic typeface to differentiate them. If using horizontal rules, the one between the headings and the body of information may look best if it is a different weight or color than the other rules.

■ Tabbing

Correctly set tabs are the backbone of a well-constructed table. If you are using numbers, consider whether the tabs should be decimal or centered; rarely will they be left or right hand tabs. (See Indents/tabs on page 96.)

■ Importing tables

When you import tables from other programs such as Microsoft Excel, they should be saved as tab-delimited text when exported. This means that each column is separated by tabs, and each row by returns, making it easy to format the imported table using the Indents/tabs feature.

If text does not appear neatly in columns when you import a tab-delimited table, you may need to select the entire text block, open Indents/tabs and set the individual tabs farther apart. Another way to solve this problem would be to decrease the point size of the text.

■ Creating fractions

Tables usually contain numerals, and numerals often contain fractions. It is not typographically correct to make a fraction that reads 1/2; better that it should read $\frac{1}{2}$. You can set up your type specifications to create a fraction like this. Here is how:

1. Open the Type specs dialog box and choose Options.

2. Enter 60 for the percentage of Super/Subscript size, 30 for the percentage of Superscript position, and 0 for the percentage of Subscript position.

3. Type the fraction, e.g., 1/2. Select the numerator (1) and make it superscript; select the denominator (2) and make it subscript. Kern the numerals until they look good. It is laborious to do this over and over; you may wish to copy a finished fraction, paste it wherever you need a fraction, select the numerator and denominator one at a time, and type in new values.

This table example is from a shipping company's service schedule. Note how its columns and rows are differentiated by color and lines.
Designer: Jim Andrews, Redwood City, CA
Client: American President Companies

From North Atlantic, Midwest, East Canada

DEPARTS

VESSEL / VOYAGE NO	POLK 21 POK	ROOSEVELT 57 FDR	ADAMS 29 ADM	MONROE 42 MON	JACKSON 30 JAX	EISENHOWER 69 IKE	TRUMAN 34 TRM	WASHINGTON 63 WAS		KENNEDY 32 JFK	LINCOLN 86 LIN	POLK 32 POK	ROOSEVELT 58 FDR	ADAMS 30 ADM	MONROE 43 MON	JACKSON 31 JAX	EISENHOWER 70 IKE	TRUMAN 35 TRM	WASHINGTON 64 WAS	KENNEDY 33 JFK	LINCOLN 86 LIN
New York/New Jersey	6-24	6-26	7-1	7-3	7-8	7-10	7-15	7-17		7-22	7-24	7-29	7-31	8-5	8-7	8-12	8-14	8-19	8-21	8-26	8-28
Baltimore	6-24	6-26	7-1	7-3	7-8	7-10	7-15	7-17		7-22	7-24	7-29	7-31	8-5	8-7	8-12	8-14	8-19	8-21	8-26	8-28
Boston	6-24	6-26	7-1	7-3	7-8	7-10	7-15	7-17		7-22	7-24	7-29	7-31	8-5	8-7	8-12	8-14	8-19	8-21	8-26	8-28
Philadelphia	6-23	6-26	9-30	7-3	7-7	7-10	7-14	7-17		7-21	7-24	7-28	7-31	8-4	8-7	8-11	8-14	8-18	8-21	8-25	8-28
Montreal	6-21	6-21	6-28	6-28	7-5	7-5	7-12	7-12		7-19	7-19	7-26	7-26	8-2	8-2	8-9	8-9	8-16	8-16	8-23	8-23
Toronto	6-21	6-21	6-28	6-28	7-5	7-5	7-12	7-12		7-19	7-19	7-26	7-26	8-2	8-2	8-9	8-9	8-16	8-16	8-23	8-23
Memphis	6-23	6-28	6-30	7-5	7-7	7-12	7-14	7-19		7-21	7-26	7-28	8-2	8-4	8-9	8-11	8-16	8-18	8-23	8-25	8-30
Chicago	6-26	6-28	7-3	7-5	7-10	7-12	7-17	7-19		7-24	7-26	7-31	8-2	8-7	8-9	8-14	8-16	8-21	8-23	8-28	8-30
Detroit	6-25	6-27	7-2	7-4	7-9	7-11	7-16	7-18		7-23	7-25	7-30	8-1	8-6	8-8	8-13	8-15	8-20	8-22	8-27	8-29
Cincinnati	6-25	6-27	7-2	7-4	7-9	7-11	7-16	7-18		7-23	7-25	7-30	8-1	8-6	8-8	8-13	8-15	8-20	8-22	8-27	8-29
Kansas City	6-25	6-27	7-2	7-4	7-9	7-11	7-16	7-18		7-23	7-25	7-30	8-1	8-6	8-8	8-13	8-15	8-20	8-22	8-27	8-29
St. Louis	6-25	6-27	7-2	7-4	7-9	7-11	7-16	7-18		7-23	7-25	7-30	8-1	8-6	8-8	8-13	8-15	8-20	8-22	8-27	8-29
San Pedro	7-2	7-2	7-9	7-10	7-16	7-17	7-23	7-24		7-30	7-31	8-6	8-7	8-13	8-14	8-20	8-21	8-27	8-28	9-3	9-4
Oakland	7-4	7-4	7-11	7-11	7-18	7-18	7-25	7-25		8-1	8-1	8-8	8-8	8-15	8-15	8-22	8-22	8-29	8-29	9-5	9-5

ARRIVES

VESSEL / VOYAGE NO	POLK 21 POK	ROOSEVELT 57 FDR	ADAMS 29 ADM	MONROE 42 MON	JACKSON 30 JAX	EISENHOWER 69 IKE	TRUMAN 34 TRM	WASHINGTON 63 WAS		KENNEDY 32 JFK	LINCOLN 86 LIN	POLK 32 POK	ROOSEVELT 58 FDR	ADAMS 30 ADM	MONROE 43 MON	JACKSON 31 JAX	EISENHOWER 70 IKE	TRUMAN 35 TRM	WASHINGTON 64 WAS	KENNEDY 33 JFK	LINCOLN 86 LIN
Japan, Korea, Hong Kong, China, Taiwan, Philippines, Guam																					
Yokohama	7-15		7-22		7-29		8-5			8-12		8-19		8-26		9-2		9-9		9-16	
Tokyo	7-16		7-23		7-30		8-6			8-13		8-20		8-27		9-3		9-10		9-17	
Nagoya	7-18		7-25		8-1		8-8			8-15		8-22		8-29		9-5		9-12		9-19	
Shimizu	7-16		7-23		7-30		8-6			8-13		8-20		8-27		9-3		9-10		9-17	
Kobe/Osaka	7-16		7-23		7-30		8-6			8-13		8-20		8-27		9-3		9-10		9-17	
Okinawa	7-29	7-22	8-5	8-5	8-12	8-12	8-19	8-19		8-26	8-26	9-2	9-2	9-9	9-9	9-16	9-16	9-23	9-23	9-30	9-30
Busan/Incheon	7-21		7-28		8-4		8-11			8-18		8-25		9-1		9-8		9-15		9-22	
Keelung	7-21	7-22	7-28	7-29	8-4	8-5	8-11	8-12		8-18	8-19	8-25	8-26	9-1	9-2	9-8	9-9	9-15	9-16	9-22	9-23
Kaohsiung	7-19	7-20	7-26	7-27	8-2	8-3	8-9	8-10		8-16	8-17	8-23	8-24	8-30	8-31	9-6	9-7	9-13	9-14	9-20	9-21
Hwangpou	7-27	7-27	8-3	8-3	8-10	8-10	8-17	8-17		8-24	8-24	8-31	8-31	9-7	9-7	9-14	9-14	9-21	9-21	9-28	9-28
Chiwan	7-28	7-28	8-4	8-4	8-11	8-11	8-18	8-18		8-25	8-25	9-1	9-1	9-8	9-8	9-15	9-15	9-22	9-22	9-29	9-29
Hong Kong	7-20	7-25	7-27	8-1	8-3	8-8	8-10	8-15		8-17	8-22	8-24	8-29	8-31	9-5	9-7	9-12	9-14	9-19	9-21	9-26
Manila	7-25	7-25	8-1	8-1	8-8	8-8	8-15	8-15		8-22	8-22	8-29	8-29	9-5	9-5	9-12	9-12	9-19	9-19	9-26	9-26
Guam/Saipan		7-15			7-22		7-29				8-12		8-19		8-26		9-2		9-9		9-16
Singapore, Malaysia, Indonesia, Thailand, Bangladesh																					
Singapore	7-25	7-25	8-1	8-1	8-8	8-8	8-15	8-15		8-22	8-22	8-29	8-29	9-5	9-5	9-12	9-12	9-19	9-19	9-26	9-26
Penang	8-1	8-1	8-8	8-8	8-15	8-15	8-22	8-22		8-29	8-29	9-5	9-5	9-12	9-12	9-19	9-19	9-26	9-26	10-3	10-3
Pt. Klang	7-30	7-30	8-6	8-6	8-13	8-13	8-20	8-20		8-27	8-27	9-3	9-3	9-10	9-10	9-17	9-17	9-24	9-24	10-1	10-1
Jakarta	8-2	8-2	8-9	8-9	8-16	8-16	8-23	8-23		8-30	8-30	9-6	9-6	9-13	9-13	9-20	9-20	9-27	9-27	10-4	10-4
Surabaya	7-31	7-31	8-7	8-7	8-14	8-14	8-21	8-21		8-28	8-28	9-4	9-4	9-11	9-11	9-18	9-18	9-25	9-25	10-2	10-2
Bangkok	7-29	7-29	8-5	8-5	8-12	8-12	8-19	8-19		8-26	8-26	9-2	9-2	9-9	9-9	9-16	9-16	9-23	9-23	9-30	9-30
Chittagong	8-1	8-1	8-8	8-8	8-15	8-15	8-22	8-22		8-29	8-29	9-5	9-5	9-12	9-12	9-19	9-19	9-26	9-26	10-3	10-3
India, Pakistan, Middle East, Sri Lanka																					
Bombay	8-10	8-10	8-17	8-17	8-24	8-24	8-31	8-31		9-7	9-7	9-14	9-14	9-21	9-21	9-28	9-28	10-5	10-5	10-12	10-12
Cochin	8-1	8-1	8-8	8-8	8-15	8-15	8-22	8-22		8-29	8-29	9-5	9-5	9-12	9-12	9-19	9-19	9-26	9-26	10-3	10-3
Madras	8-1	8-1	8-8	8-8	8-15	8-15	8-22	8-22		8-29	8-29	9-5	9-5	9-12	9-12	9-19	9-19	9-26	9-26	10-3	10-3
Calcutta	8-2	8-2	8-9	8-9	8-16	8-16	8-23	8-23		8-30	8-30	9-5	9-5	9-13	9-13	9-20	9-20	9-27	9-27	10-4	10-4
Karachi	8-5	8-5	8-12	8-12	8-19	8-19	8-26	8-26		9-2	9-2	9-9	9-9	9-16	9-16	9-23	9-23	9-30	9-30	10-7	10-7
Muscat	8-4	8-4			8-18	8-18				9-1	9-1			9-15	9-15			9-29	9-29		
Dammam	8-9	8-9	8-16	8-16	8-23	8-23	8-30	8-30		9-6	9-6	9-13	9-13	9-20	9-20	9-27	9-27	10-4	10-4	10-11	10-11
Kuwait	8-12	8-12	8-19	8-19	8-26	8-26	9-2	9-2		9-9	9-9	9-16	9-16	9-23	9-23	9-30	9-30	10-7	10-7	10-14	10-14
Bahrain	8-8	8-8	8-15	8-15	8-22	8-22	8-29	8-29		9-5	9-5	9-12	9-12	9-19	9-19	9-26	9-26	10-3	10-3	10-10	10-10
Riyadh	8-13	8-13	8-20	8-20	8-27	8-27	9-3	9-3		9-10	9-10	9-17	9-17	9-24	9-24	10-1	10-1	10-8	10-8	10-15	10-15
Doha/Sharjah/Abu Dhabi	8-4	8-4	8-11	8-11	8-18	8-18	8-25	8-25		9-1	9-1	9-8	9-8	9-15	9-15	9-22	9-22	9-29	9-29	10-6	10-6
Fujairah/Jebel Ali	8-2	8-2	8-9	8-9	8-16	8-16	8-23	8-23		8-30	8-30	9-6	9-6	9-13	9-13	9-20	9-20	9-27	9-27	10-4	10-4
Dubai	8-3	8-3	8-10	8-10	8-17	8-17	8-24	8-24		8-31	8-31	9-7	9-7	9-14	9-14	9-21	9-21	9-28	9-28	10-5	10-5
Colombo	7-29	7-29	8-5	8-5	8-12	8-12	8-19	8-19		8-26	8-26	9-2	9-2	9-9	9-9	9-16	9-16	9-23	9-23	9-30	9-30
Australia																					
Sydney	8-10		8-14		8-21		8-28			9-4		9-11		9-18		9-25		10-2		10-9	
Melbourne	8-14		8-21		8-28		9-4			9-11		9-18		9-25		10-2		10-9		10-16	

Containership Service   Stacktrain Service   Truck Service

Color

Red excites and makes us hungry. Yellow warns, and grabs for attention. Blue says integrity, dignity. Green is pastoral and reassuring and can invoke feelings of envy. Purple is royal; orange is hot.

Color is one of the most important design elements. It can be used to create a mood, attract attention, differentiate various sections of a publication, or tie multiple sections together. Think about what individual colors say, and assess how they work together when combined on a page.

Color methods

Designing and producing publications in color adds new levels of complexity to the page layout process. It must be approached with careful planning. Costs double or quadruple when two, four, or more pages of imagesetting, film, and plates for each printed page must be rerun because of a mistake. This makes proofreading, measurement, assignment of screen values, correct font identification, linking image files, and other production steps very important.

There are two methods for setting up a publication to print in color: spot color and process color. Spot color requires the use of a separate ink for each color you print. Process color uses four specified inks to produce the whole spectrum of color through a combination of screens. The method you use depends on several factors: your budget, the effect you wish to achieve, and the type of artwork the client provides.

Choosing colors

Swatch books are available from companies such as Pantone, Trumatch, Focaltone and others, for both spot color and process color. For spot color, there are Pantone® books to show the hundreds of ink colors that can be created by mixing to a pre-set formula in the Pantone Matching System (PMS). These books come in small selector decks that fan out and have colors printed on both coated and uncoated papers. There are also specifier versions that have multiple chips of each color so they can be torn out and attached to mock-ups or paper samples to show clients or printers how the color will look.

Tint selectors show how various colors in screen levels—from 10% to 80%—look when printed; two color selectors show the result when two different colors are mixed; color and black selectors show the effect of black in combination with popular colors; and black colors and effects books show effects from the use of twelve different black tints.

For process color printing, the Trumatch Colorfinder books show hundreds of colors that can be created using combinations of percentages of the four process colors, cyan, magenta, yellow and black. (Pages 40-43 of this book contain formulas for creating colors based on CMYK.)

The Trumatch color selector.

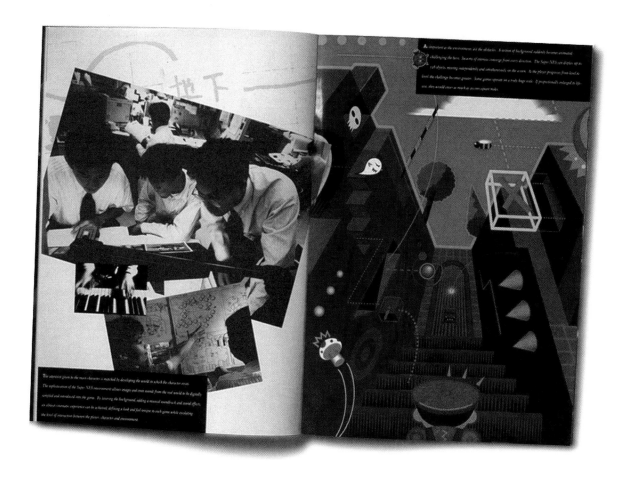

The extravagant use of color in this annual
report ranges from duotone photos on the
left-hand page, to the vibrant illustration
on the right.
Designer: Dorothy A. Cross, Leimer Cross
Design, Seattle
Client: Nintendo Company, Ltd.

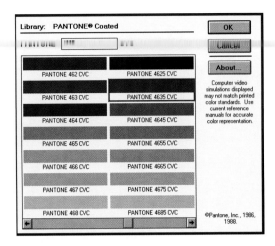

Accessing the submenu "Libraries" yields a selection of choices. These represent different color specification models for both spot and process color selection.

Color libraries in PageMaker

PageMaker's color handling begins with color libraries accessed through the Define colors command under the Element menu. As seen in the menu to the left, they include several spot and process color libraries. When you want to make a library available in PageMaker's color palette, choose the color you want from a swatch book (never use the screen display to judge color accuracy) and follow these steps:

1. Choose Define colors from the Element menu.

2. Click New, and then select Spot, Process or Tint. Choose which color model you want to use, RGB, HLS or CMYK. (Use CMYK for publications that will be commercially printed, and RGB for those that will be imaged to slides.)

3. Click on the arrow to the right of Libraries to display the selection of library choices and release the mouse on the library name you want to use.

4. Type a value for the library color number, or scroll through the library until you find the color you want to add. Click OK.

5. Choose whether or not the color should overprint other colors in the publication. (See Overprinting, page 48.)

6. Click on the OK button to close dialog boxes, and the color's name will be added, in alphabetical order, to the color palette.

This screen capture shows an array of choices displayed as you scroll through the Pantone library.

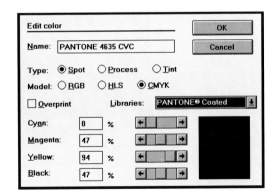

After you have selected a Pantone color to add to the Color palette, this screen appears. At this stage, you can create a tint of that Pantone color.

Spot Color

For the simplest color work—spot color—the printer mixes colored ink based on a formula. If you want a line of text and some boxes to be red, you supply the printer with numbers for the particular color of red you have chosen, two pieces of camera-ready art (one for black, one for red), and a tissue overlay or laser prints indicating which elements should print which color. You can use just one piece of camera-ready art if the two colors don't touch anywhere. When colors touch or one overprints another, two pieces of art (or separations) must be supplied. The printer prepares separate plates for the red and black inks.

Generally, use of more than three spot colors in a project is as expensive as full-color process printing. Unless there is a valid design reason—such as matching a company's logo colors perfectly, achieving vibrancy and intense clarity of color, or a requirement for special inks such as metallics or fluorescents—opt for process color when you require three or four different colors.

Designing with spot color

When using spot color, the guiding principle should be consistency. If one headline is in color, all headlines should be in the same color. Screened backgrounds in a color should not vary from one page to another without a specific reason for doing so.

Here are some design techniques that can be used with spot color:

■ Use the second color for a graphic under the text.

■ Use the second color for drop caps, headlines, lead-in text, or other styles.

■ Create screened rectangles in a spot color for backgrounds.

■ Use percentages of black ink in conjunction with the colored ink to make a third color.

■ Print percentages in black ink under the colored ink to create additional shades of color.

Text in a spot color

When you want to print text in a second color, select the letters, words, or paragraphs with the Text tool (in either Story Edit or Layout view). Click on your color choice in the color palette and the text will appear in the new color onscreen. When you print the file, clicking Separations (found in the Color section of the Print dialog box) will give you the capability to choose separations if your print job requires them.

Graphical elements in a spot color

If your graphical elements are drawn in PageMaker, they will display the color attributes that you assign to them. If, however, they are imported from other programs, such as Aldus FreeHand, you will not see the PageMaker assigned color onscreen. Note that if you are using a spot color (for example, Pantone 450) in PageMaker, and want to print an EPS graphic in that color, you can place a line drawing or gray-scale drawing in EPS format that is black, and assign it the second color in the Color palette. Though the screen display will not show the graphic in color, it will print in the second color. If you want to print the graphic in black and the spot color, you must assign the colors in your graphics program.

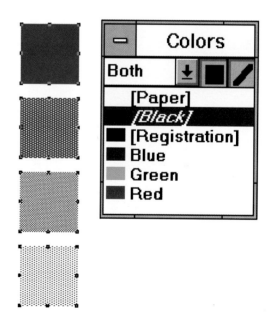

The squares at the right, all of which have been assigned the same color from the color palette, have been assigned different percentage screen fills under the Element, Fill menu.

Special spot colors

Spot colors that also add impact to any publication are fluorescents, pastels, and metallics. There are swatch books and specifiers for these colors that show the range of variations that you can achieve with these inks.

Two or more spot colors

Most often, a two-color publication features black for text, and a second color for graphics, rules, and other elements. It is not much more expensive to print with two colors instead of black and a color. If chosen carefully, different screen percentages of two colors can be combined to yield a different third color.

Guidelines for spot color in PageMaker

It does not matter what colors appear on screen if you are using the spot color model for separation; simply ensure that items printing in the second color are identified as a color other than black. The color palette in default mode already lists Paper, Black, Registration, Blue, Red and Green as color choices. In order to assign a color to an element, you must have that element selected and the color palette open. Although it is possible to set up a publication specifying the actual number(s) of the Pantone or other color model, it is not necessary to do so if you are using spot rather than process color separation. You can use any of PageMaker's default colors (Red, Blue, Green) to specify color items. This is particularly useful if you have not made a final decision about which spot color you want to use. Rather than specifying PMS 547 for the blue your client has not yet approved, use the default Blue to select all the items that appear in blue. This way, if and when your client chooses a different color of blue at the last minute, you won't run the risk of having a wrong PMS number output on the bottom of the high-resolution film. That would cause confusion for the printer.

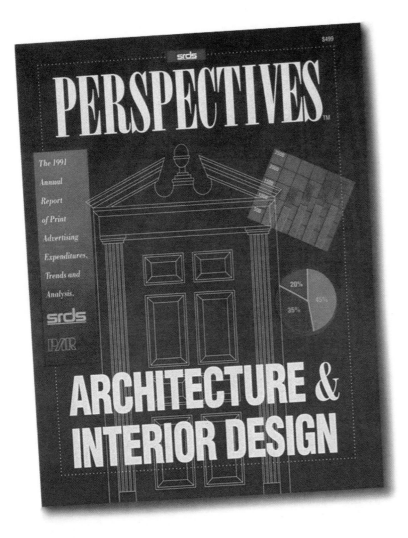

The cover at the left shows the use of two spot colors, blue and magenta. When mixed, they form a range of purple colors.
Designer: Beth Bast, Beth Bast Designs, Chicago
Client: SRDS

Process color

Process color is the printing of any color or range of colors by mixing them from a combination of different levels of four basic process inks: cyan, magenta, yellow, and black (CMYK). A color separation is a breakdown of a full-color photograph or other art into four process color components, performed by electronic or mechanical means. Metal or paper printing plates are made from each of these four elements, and as they are printed in registration, one after another, they result in a full-color approximation of the original photo or illustration.

PageMaker 5.0 can perform process color separations when outputting final pages on a high-resolution imagesetter—or on a laser printer for proofing purposes. If you have scanned or drawn color graphics in your document, the program breaks those graphics down into their cyan, magenta, yellow and black components when you choose Separations in the Color section of the Print dialog box (See below).

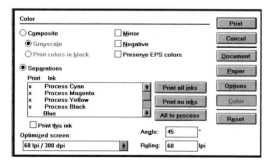

When it's time to print your document, you can choose whether to print composite or separations.

Designing with process color

Using process color increases the complexity of your project by geometric proportions. There is so much to know about color printing, and so much that can go wrong if you make a mistake, that it may be better to supply your printer with the color photographs or graphics you want to use, and have them stripped in conventionally. Still, there are times when that is an extra challenge because you are using color backgrounds, color type, or other techniques.

When using four-color process printing, the tremendous choice of colors gives you many design options. Part of the challenge at hand is to narrow down those options.

- Get a Trumatch book or other process color selector and select a range of colors to serve as your basic palette. Or, you can choose color formulas from the following pages.

- If you have a Pantone spot color selector, you can choose the colors from that library in PageMaker, but they will be CMYK equivalents when separated—not as vibrant and not true to the color chips in the book.

- You can create backgrounds, just as you can with spot color. Assigning different screen values to them will make them lighter or darker.

- If you want to use blends or gradient fills of different colors, you will need to create them in programs such as Aldus FreeHand, Aldus PhotoStyler, Adobe Illustrator, or Adobe Photoshop, and import them into PageMaker.

Text in process color

You can assign any color you wish to text in process color, but it is not a good idea for small point sizes. This is because printing plates or paper may shift in commercial printing—especially true on a web press—and one or more colors may print out of register. This can yield red type with a yellow "halo"—hard to read and messy looking.

Graphical elements in process color

If you are using process color, try to avoid very thin rules—for the same reason as small point sizes of type—misregistration in printing may cause blurring.

Imported scans of color photographs or illustrations are broken down automatically into their CMYK components when you use PageMaker for separation. Scans must be CMYK TIFF or PCS, not RGB TIFF files.

OVERVIEW

39

CMYK formulas

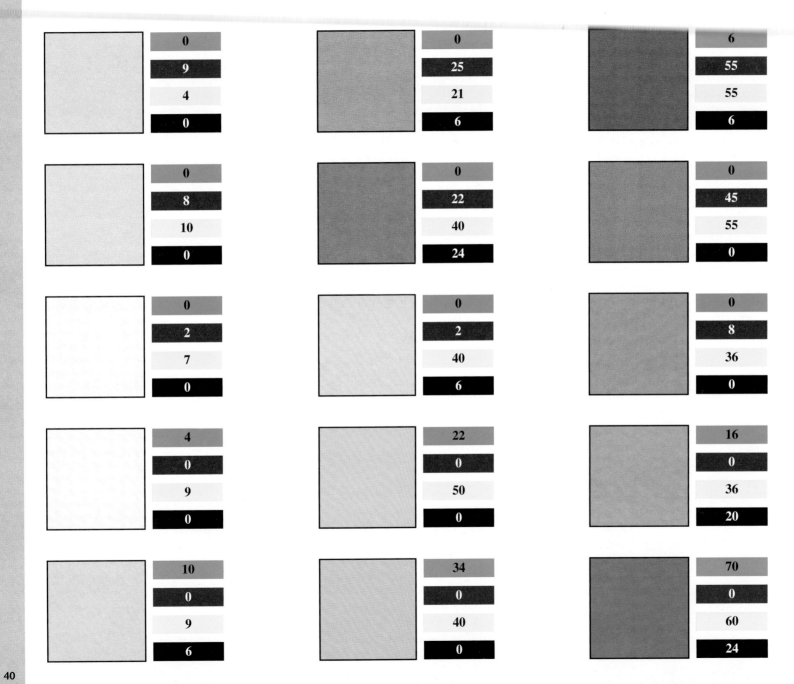

	C	M	Y	K
	0	9	4	0
	0	8	10	0
	0	2	7	0
	4	0	9	0
	10	0	9	6
	0	25	21	6
	0	22	40	24
	0	2	40	6
	22	0	50	0
	34	0	40	0
	6	55	55	6
	0	45	55	0
	0	8	36	0
	16	0	36	20
	70	0	60	24

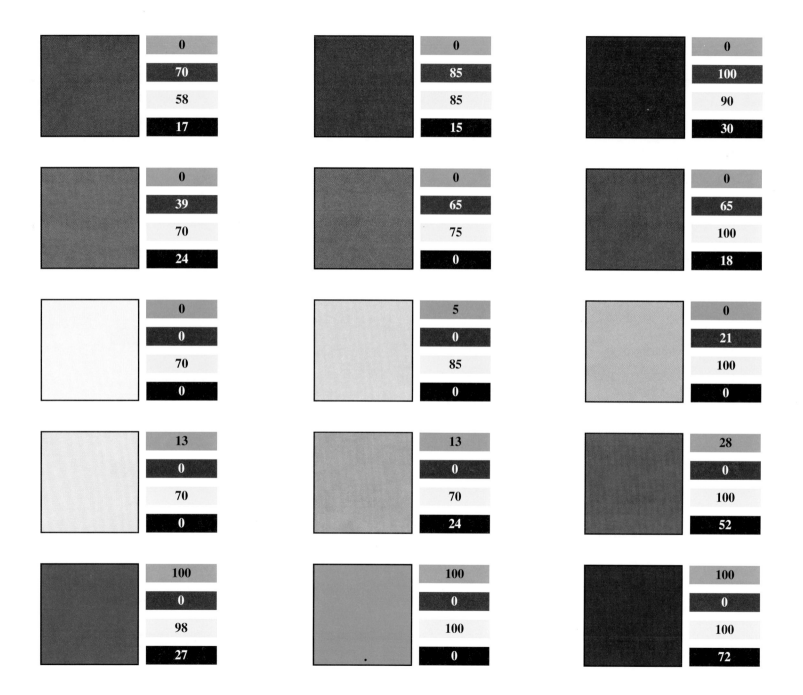

0	0	0	
70	85	100	
58	85	90	
17	15	30	
0	0	0	
39	65	65	
70	75	100	
24	0	18	
0	5	0	
0	0	21	
70	85	100	
0	0	0	
13	13	28	
0	0	0	
70	70	100	
0	24	52	
100	100	100	
0	0	0	
98	100	100	
27	0	72	

CMYK formulas

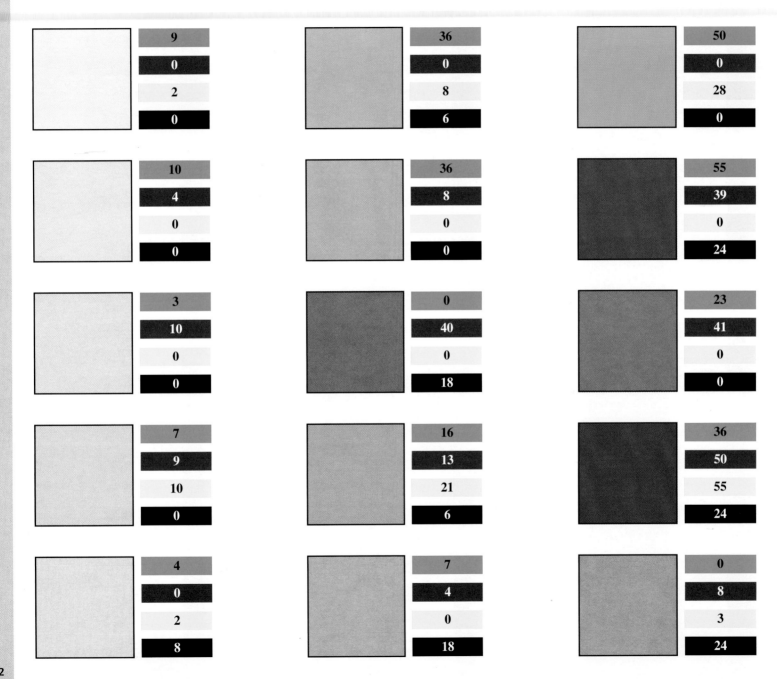

Row 1: 9 / 0 / 2 / 0 — 36 / 0 / 8 / 6 — 50 / 0 / 28 / 0

Row 2: 10 / 4 / 0 / 0 — 36 / 8 / 0 / 0 — 55 / 39 / 0 / 24

Row 3: 3 / 10 / 0 / 0 — 0 / 40 / 0 / 18 — 23 / 41 / 0 / 0

Row 4: 7 / 9 / 10 / 0 — 16 / 13 / 21 / 6 — 36 / 50 / 55 / 24

Row 5: 4 / 0 / 2 / 8 — 7 / 4 / 0 / 18 — 0 / 8 / 3 / 24

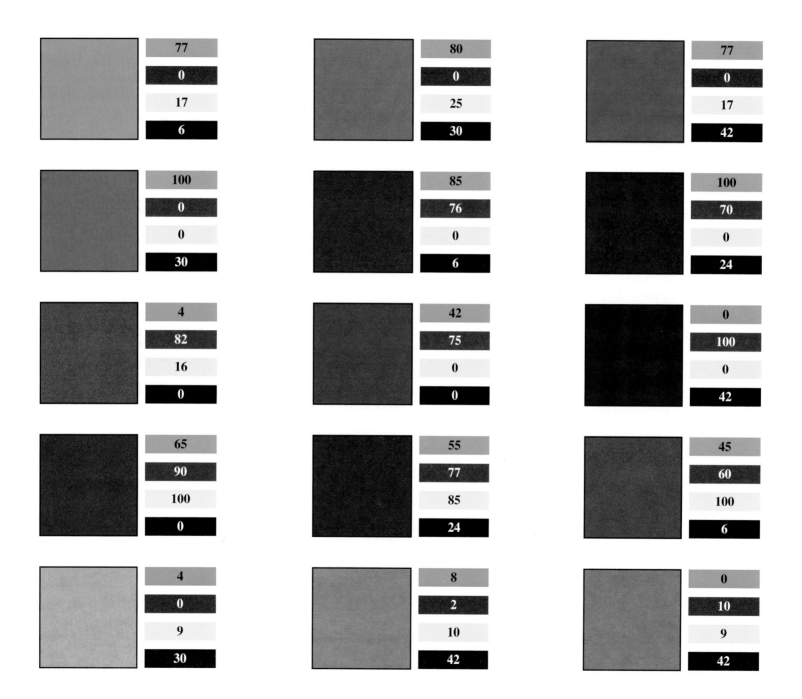

	77
	0
	17
	6

	80
	0
	25
	30

	77
	0
	17
	42

	100
	0
	0
	30

	85
	76
	0
	6

	100
	70
	0
	24

	4
	82
	16
	0

	42
	75
	0
	0

	0
	100
	0
	42

	65
	90
	100
	0

	55
	77
	85
	24

	45
	60
	100
	6

	4
	0
	9
	30

	8
	2
	10
	42

	0
	10
	9
	42

Using color libraries with process color

You can choose from any or all of the color libraries if you are printing in process color. Make rules, screens, and other graphics any color you can find or create under the Define colors command. If you fill a box with a Trumatch blue-green with a specific number, when you go to final output, the program can separate that fill, break it down into percentages of cyan, magenta, yellow and black that when combined will closely match the color you selected from the book.

Automatic color separation

One concern about PageMaker, before 5.0, was that you had to run pages through Aldus PrePrint if you wanted them color separated. This was inconvenient and required opening another application. With version 5.0, it is no longer necessary to use PrePrint for most color separations, because colors separate within PageMaker itself.

The TIFF scan at the right is printed as a color monotone. Even though it appears to be just one color, it is made up of percentages of cyan, magenta, yellow, and black.

Even though PageMaker will color separate full color photographs, consider printing some photos as color monotones to achieve a more graphical effect. This can be done as follows:

1. If your scan is full-color, either rescan the image as gray-scale and save in TIFF format, or reopen it in an image processing program such as Adobe Photoshop and convert it to gray-scale.

2. Place the scan into PageMaker with the Place command under the File menu.

3. With the image selected, choose a color from the color palette.

4. When color separation takes place, the image appears to be a monotone (various levels of one color), even though the one color it is made up of will be composed of different amounts of Cyan, Magenta, Yellow, and Black.

The Color Palette

You can find the color palette under the Window menu. A description of each element of the color palette follows:

■ **Palette menu**

A color selection can be made to include both the fill and surrounding line of an element, the fill only, or the line only. Clicking on either the square or the diagonal line to the right of the word, selects an object's fill or its line, if you have selected the object.

■ **Paper color**

When you make any element this "color," objects that are behind it will not print where the paper colored element overlaps them. If your document is to be printed on a colored paper, it is possible to see how that paper will look (onscreen) by editing the color of [Paper]:

1. Choose Edit Color under the Element menu.

2. Select [Paper]. Click on Edit.

3. Select a new color for [Paper] that looks like the color of paper you will be printing on.

4. Click on the OK button and the background of your document will change to that color. When you print the document to a laser printer or imagesetter, the color of the paper does not print.

■ **Black**

[Black] must be assigned to text or other elements with care. Like other PageMaker colors, Black knocks out by default. The difference is that text colored 100% Black overprints by default. You cannot edit the default Black, so if you want a black that overprints objects, follow this procedure:

1. Choose Define colors from the Element menu.

2. Click New.

3. Name your new black "Black 2" or something similar to distinguish it from default [Black];

4. Click Tint.

5. Select the base color [Black].

6. Click Overprint.

7. Make sure tint is set at 100%.

8. Click on the OK button.

If you do this, make sure any black elements you wish to overprint are changed from the default black to your new black.

■ **Registration**

Choose the Registration option when an item must print on all separations. For instance, crop marks that you have drawn yourself, registration marks, or job identification information such as file names, creator names, etc. This option should not be confused with PageMaker's printer marks, also known as Registration marks.

■ **Blue, Green and Red**

Blue, Green and Red are default colors in the program, and if you have chosen specific colors from a library, you may want to remove these. This is easy to accomplish following this procedure:

1. Choose Define colors from the Element menu.

2. Select Red, Blue or Green.

3. Click on Remove.

4. Click on the OK button.

If you attempt to remove a color and have previously assigned an element that color, PageMaker 5.0 will ask if you want to change all elements in that color to [Black].

Four-color black

There is black—and there is really black. When using four-color process printing, you may want to add a four-color black. Four-color black has a depth that cannot be found simply by printing one pass of black ink. Instead, it combines all four colors at 100%. You can see in the example below how four-color black is different from plain black. (Never use four-color black for type because it creates registration problems. For backgrounds and other graphics, it works very well.) Here is how to make it:

1. Choose Define colors from the Element menu.

2. Select New.

3. Choose CMYK; type in the name 4-color black to distinguish it from regular black, and select 100% for black, and 60% for Cyan, Magenta, and Yellow.

4. Click on the OK button.

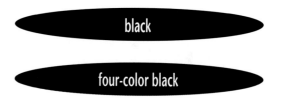

Combining process and spot color

If you have a large printing budget, you may want to use more than four colors. It is not unusual to specify five or even six colors—for example, CMYK, a Pantone color, and a spot varnish. Any more than six colors will require a specialized printing press.

When you use a fifth color, it can be applied as a premixed ink, or as a CMYK combination with PageMaker 5.0, you can designate whether individual colors should be treated as process, or spot, when outputting the files. Confusion may occur when you use Pantone or other color library formulas in a document printed in process color. The color libraries contain formulas for color separation to CMYK for objects designated by a Color-curve, DaiNippon, Pantone, or Toyo spot color. Spot colors are broken down into their process equivalents. The process equivalents of pre-mixed ink colors are rarely exact matches. If you want to make a strong impact with a particular color, consider printing it as a fifth, spot color.

Color effects

There are two easy ways to add color to any publication, even if you are only printing in black.

One of the least expensive methods is to print on colored paper. Combining different colors for separate pages can be effective if the colors are complementary. Call paper suppliers in your region and ask them for sample books, or sample sheets of a particular paper you have in mind. Find out whether the paper is in stock or if it requires special ordering. Usually only the largest print runs justify the quantities suppliers require to place a special order.

Another way to get a sense of color into a publication being printed in black only, is to think of white, black, and the levels of grays as colors. With its screening capabilities, PageMaker 5.0 can provide a wide array of gray choices for any page. Using the range of grays effectively is a challenge for any designer, and can result in distinctive and handsome documents. Don't be heavy-handed. Seek subtlety and rhythm, balance, and contrast in your use of grays and they will add color to your pages.

There are various screen values found under the Fill menu, but they are limited to 10% increments and cannot be applied to type or lines. You can make any text or object print in a much wider range of gray levels by creating your own gray colors. Follow these steps:

1. Choose Define colors from the Element menu.

2. Select [Black], and choose New to create an additional color.

3. Set Black level to any percentage between 1% and 99%. (It is difficult for many printing processes to hold screens below 10%, or for any screen values higher than 90% to be distinguishable from black.)

4. Name your new color, (e.g., 25% black) and click on the OK button. The name is added in alphabetical order to the color palette as a choice, and you can select that color for type or graphics.

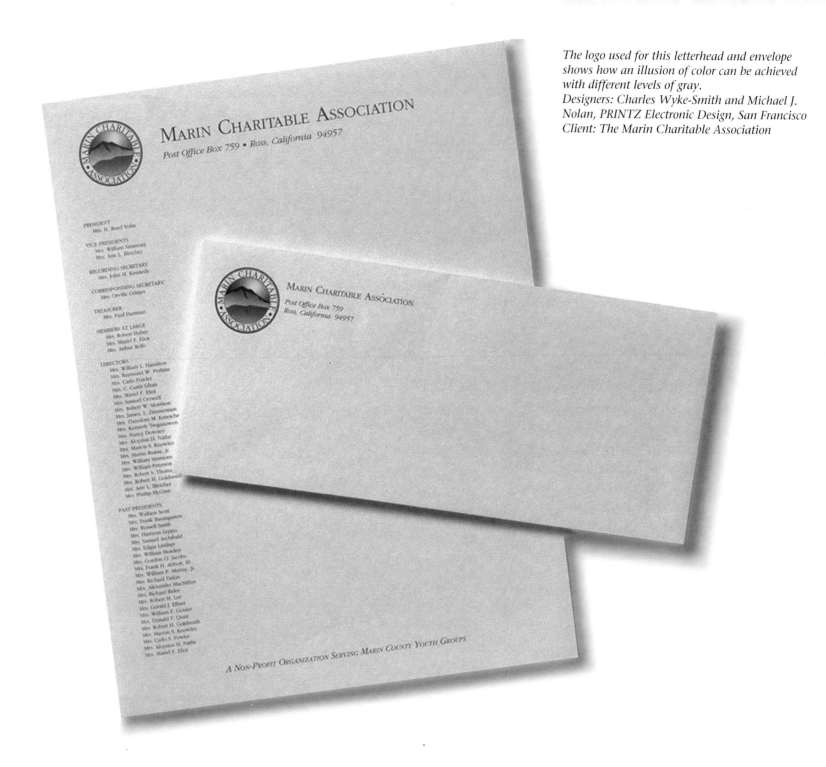

The logo used for this letterhead and envelope shows how an illusion of color can be achieved with different levels of gray.
Designers: Charles Wyke-Smith and Michael J. Nolan, PRINTZ Electronic Design, San Francisco
Client: The Marin Charitable Association

MARIN CHARITABLE ASSOCIATION

Post Office Box 759 • Ross, California 94957

PRESIDENT
Mrs. H. Reed Volin

VICE PRESIDENTS
Mrs. William Simmons
Mrs. Arie L. Bleicher

RECORDING SECRETARY
Mrs. John M. Kennedy

CORRESPONDING SECRETARY
Mrs. Orville Grimes

TREASURER
Mrs. Paul Hartman

MEMBERS AT LARGE
Mrs. Robert Huber
Mrs. Mariel F. Eliot
Mrs. Arthur Belfe

DIRECTORS
Mrs. William L. Hamilton
Mrs. Raymond W. Perkins
Mrs. Carlo Fowler
Mrs. C. Curtis Ghan
Mrs. Mariel F. Eliot
Mrs. Samuel Crowell
Mrs. Robert W. Morrison
Mrs. James L. Zimmerman
Mrs. Theodore M. Knieische
Mrs. Kenneth Teegaeowen
Mrs. Nancy Downey
Mrs. Aloysius H. Nathe
Mrs. Marvin S. Knowles
Mrs. Martin Buane, Jr.
Mrs. William Simmons
Mrs. William Peterson
Mrs. Robert S. Thoma
Mrs. Robert H. Goldsmith
Mrs. Arie L. Bleicher
Mrs. Phillip McGinn

PAST PRESIDENTS
Mrs. Wallace Scott
Mrs. Frank Baumgarten
Mrs. Russell Smith
Mrs. Harrison Lepps
Mrs. Samuel Archibald
Mrs. Edgar Lindner
Mrs. William Mosden
Mrs. Gordon O. Jacobs
Mrs. Frank H. Abbott, III
Mrs. William P. Murray, Jr.
Mrs. Richard Dakin
Mrs. Alexander MacMillan
Mrs. Richard Rider
Mrs. Robert M. Lee
Mrs. Gerald J. Elbert
Mrs. William F. Genler
Mrs. Donald F. Quist
Mrs. Robert H. Goldsmith
Mrs. Marion S. Knowles
Mrs. Carlo S. Fowler
Mrs. Aloysius H. Nathe
Mrs. Mariel F. Eliot

A NON-PROFIT ORGANIZATION SERVING MARIN COUNTY YOUTH GROUPS

MARIN CHARITABLE ASSOCIATION
Post Office Box 759
Ross, California 94957

Overprinting

The questions posed by overprinting can be confusing for many people. When using two colors, the darker color is generally printed after the lighter one. This means that black text appearing on a yellow box will be printed on top of the box. If you are printing blue text on a yellow box, you could get a color mix of green text. To avoid this mix, you can make sure the text knocks out of the box below it. That means the camera-ready art for the yellow layer will show the type reversed out. To further complicate matters, items that don't overprint generally need to be trapped. (See Trapping, page 49.)

In PageMaker 5.0, all colors are set to knock-out by default unless you have selected Overprint. One exception is 100% Black text in Pagemaker 5.0 which overprints by default. You can specify that individual PageMaker-drawn elements overprint. For example, if you want a red circle to knock out of the black box that surrounds it, place a 1 point red rule around the circle that overprints, so misregistration while printing does not create a white gap anywhere. This is known as object-level overprinting.

If you want certain attributes of a PageMaker-drawn object to overprint, here is how it works:

1. Select the object with the Pointer tool.

2. Choose Fill and line... from the Element menu.

3. Choose the colors you want for fill and line.

4. Indicate if you want the line or fill to print over the object(s) placed behind it. If you do not choose Overprint, the fill or line will knock out the objects behind it.

5. Click on the OK button.

If you wish to make a color—and all objects assigned to that color—overprint rather than knock out, here is how to do it:

1. Choose Define colors from the Elements menu.

2. Select the existing color you wish to use for overprinting.

3. Click Edit. Click the overprint option. Click OK. Click OK again to exit Define colors.

If you want some objects in a color to over-print, and other objects in the same color to knock out, here's how that's done:

1. Choose Define colors (Control-3).

2. Click New.

3. Type the name of the new color that distinguishes it as the knock out color (Blue K/O).

4. Click Tint.

5. Choose the base color.

6. Be sure Overprint is not selected.

7. Make the percentage 100.

8. Click OK and OK again to exit Define colors.

Trapping

Trapping is a production issue that may cause confusion. While the concept is simple to understand, it can be difficult to achieve consistent results. Trapping is the overlapping of separate colors that prevent gaps during the printing process. Trapping is one of those printer's arts, developed and refined over decades, that has only recently fallen into the lap of the designer through the power of electronic publishing. For that reason, it makes more sense to leave trapping to the experts—commercial printers—rather than attempt it yourself.

Trapping is necessary because different colors of ink are not laid down at the same time on the printing press. They are printed in succession. While a good commercial printer makes every attempt to keep all plates in registration, many factors—such as paper expansion or shrinkage, temperature, ink coverage, and so forth—may cause misregistration. When that happens, one color prints out of alignment with the others, and gaps may appear where the colors were supposed to meet. To prevent gaps, trapping was developed to slightly overlap colors where they touch.

These pages present only a brief overview of trapping so that you can understand its implications. You should talk to your commercial printer about trapping before you get too far into the development of your project. It is also important to talk to your service bureau and get advice as well.

Here is some information about trapping you should know:

- Trapping is generally most important with spot color jobs where different colors overlap each other.

- Trapping is more of an issue if your job printed on a high-speed web press, less so on a sheet-fed press.

- There are two terms used commonly for traps: spread and choke. Spread means that a stroke is added to an inner, lighter color. Choke is when a stroke (overprinting line) is added to the inner edge of a surrounding, lighter color.

- Your commercial printer often can compensate for potential trapping problems by exposing film slightly longer when making plates. This process subtly increasing the width of lines. Don't assume that this will be the case; talk to the printer.

- Your service bureau may be able to effect excellent trapping using additional software such as Aldus TrapWise, rather than you performing the trapping.

Page layout

PageMaker is a page layout program that covers a number of functions. This section discusses basic page considerations, such as what size paper you use, the use of master pages, setting up a grid, automatic page numbering, sorting page order, setting up pages for bleeds, and so forth.

The size of the page below is indicated by the pair of shoes at the bottom of it. PageMaker can be used to create pages that will print this large or larger; it's just a matter of planning.
Designer: Ron Louie, Pentagram Design, New York
Client: Cactus

50

Page sizes

If the publication is something the reader can display, such as a poster or calendar, an over-size page may be necessary. If you want the reader to file the document for further reference, it is important that it fit into a file folder. If you are designing a card or invitation, be certain there are envelopes already made that it will fit into snugly. If it is to be kept in a pocket or wallet, it must be small enough to do so.

Choose a page size that allows printing on standard sizes of paper and printing presses— or be prepared to pay a premium.

Standard paper sizes

Odd page sizes can mean waste and extra cost. Before you choose a page size, determine the size sheet your job will be printed on. Also determine how to best utilize the sheet to eliminate the amount lost to trimming. Consult your printer on this matter because various printing presses use different sizes of paper.

- 8 $^1/_2$" x 11"
- 11" x 17"
- 23" x 35"
- 24" x 36"
- 25" x 35"
- 25" x 38"
- 35" x 45"
- 38" x 50"

Standard page trims

There are some standard trimmed page sizes that correspond to the sizes paper comes in. For instance, 24 individual sheets of 4" x 9" can be cut from a single sheet of 24" x 36" paper. Some of the most common are:

- 4" x 9"
- 4 $^1/_4$" x 5 $^3/_8$"
- 4 $^1/_2$" x 6"
- 5 $^1/_2$" x 8 $^1/_2$"
- 6" x 9"
- 8 $^1/_2$" x 11"
- 9" x 12"

Standard envelopes

It is expensive to have envelopes custom-made—and also just the kind of time-consuming work that may throw a project off schedule if the need comes as a surprise at the last minute. Therefore, it is usually best to design with standard sizes and types of envelopes in mind. Some of the standard sizes (and their shorthand names) are as follows:

- No. 6   3 $^3/_8$" x 6"
- No. 10   4 $^1/_8$" x 9 $^1/_2$ "
- No. 9 $^1/_2$
  (Booklet)   9" x 12"
- No. 13   10" x 13"
- A-2   4 $^3/_8$" x 5 $^5/_8$ "
- A-6   4 $^3/_4$" x 6 $^1/_2$ "
- A-7   5 $^1/_4$" x 7 $^1/_4$ "
- A-8   5 $^1/_2$" x 8 $^1/_8$ "
- A-10   6 $^1/_4$" x 9 $^5/_8$ "

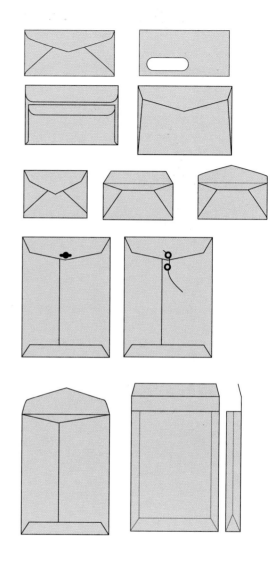

The diagrams above show different envelope types, from commercial on the top left to window, announcement, catalog, booklet, and expandable styles.

Page sizes that get attention

Sometimes, page size is dictated by the need to grab attention. If that is the case, consider a very small or very large page. Shapes grab attention, too. A square page makes an unusual statement and is quite easy to work with. A diagonal trim prior to folding can add variation to an invitation or brochure.

Non-standard page sizes

For projects such as a letterhead or business cards, it is necessary to adhere to standards. Business cards should always be 2" by 3 1/2" because many people who receive them file them in standard card holders or other files. (This does not mean that they cannot have clever flaps, folds, die cuts, or other creative devices.) Letterhead must fit into typewriters, printers, or envelopes and should always be 8 1/2" x 11".

Folding options

Folding by a printer requires planning. Although the printer usually performs the task by machine, you should hand-fold sample sheets of the paper the publication will be printed on. This gives you a feel for the folding characteristics. For instance, does one side look different than the other? Is the grain in the wrong direction? Does it need to be scored by the printer before it is folded? Talk to your printer about the folding and make sure it is included in the bid.

There are many ways to fold paper. Folds are an integral part of the design. Plan for, and around, folds and make the most of them. They can be treated as an invisible element, or they can be used to define sections or pages. Unique folds can be part of the "hook" of any publication. Here is some information you need to know about folding:

- There are two basic kinds of folds, parallel and right angle. It is also possible to fold at an angle, but this is difficult and requires handwork by the printer.

- If you are using a heavy paper stock, it probably will need to be scored before it is folded. Pay particular attention to scoring if your paper stock is coated, a foil, a duplex, or other specialty.

- Trimming, scoring, perforating, pasting, and slitting can all be done with attachments to a folding machine.

- Panels can be created through different types of parallel and right angle folds: four, six, eight, twelve, and sixteen pages.

This striking self-promotion piece for a design firm makes the most of both unusual page size and folding.
Design by: Bay Graphics, Berkeley, CA

A quick measurement for folds

If you are setting up a number of folds on a large page, you can quickly measure where the fold lines should be—even if you have complicated margins:

1. Temporarily change the page setup so that the margin measurement is zero in all categories. (You may want to jot down the margin specifications if they are complex, because you will need to reenter them later.)

2. Go to the master pages and change column guides to the number of folds you wish to use. Specify 0 for column width.

3. Draw ruler guides out to the column markers from the Ruler.

4. Change Page Setup back to the original specifications. Now viewing any page reflects both the new margins and accurate, pre-measured fold lines.

Indicating fold lines

If you are using a common fold (such as fold in thirds), it is usually not necessary for you to indicate on the final artwork where the fold lines should be. However, if you are going to trim your page, or intend to have overlapping or uneven folds, you must indicate where they should be. Fold marks are very easy to make with PageMaker using the following steps:

1. Make sure you are on the master page.

2. Drag a ruler guide to where you want the fold.

3. Choose the line tool and specify a dotted line from the Element/Line menu.

4. Select Registration from the color palette. Lines will appear on the artwork for all colors when separated.

5. Draw a dotted line that just touches the edge of the page and extends $1/4"$ beyond the edge. The line prints in final imagesetting, but will not interfere with artwork that bleeds. (If it does interfere, the printer probably can mask it out later.)

6. Copy and power paste (Control-Shift-P), the dotted line. Holding down the Shift key, drag the pasted line to the other edge of the page.

7. Copy and power paste both lines; shift-drag them to the next fold.

Indicating crop lines

If you want an unusual trim—such as an angle, you must indicate the crop marks manually, rather than using PageMaker's automatic crop marks feature.

1. On the master page, use horizontal and vertical ruler guides to define the four sides of your trimmed page.

2. Choose a .5 pt solid line and Registration from the color palette.

3. $1/4"$ to the left of the left-hand vertical ruler guide, draw a $1/2"$ horizontal line along the top measurement. Copy, power paste, and shift-drag the pasted line to the bottom horizontal measurement.

4. Copy and power paste both lines, and shift drag them until they are $1/4"$ to the right of the right-hand vertical measurement line.

5. Repeat the process for vertical trim lines.

Master pages

Master pages should be the first pages you work on when you open a new document. They are where you build your grid, set automatic page numbering, create common headers and footers, folding marks, and similar elements that will repeat throughout the document.

Items placed on master pages may be displayed on the individual pages of your document. Choose Display master items under the Layout menu, which acts as an on/off toggle switch.

You can change guidelines on individual pages, and then by choosing the Copy master guides command under the Layout menu, restore the original master guides.

Establishing the grid

A grid is an invisible division of the page into equal, measured parts. Think of a grid as you would the ironwork for a tall building—necessary to ensure a beautiful structure. Of course, the grid can be broken when you choose to do so, but unless it is there to begin with, you cannot achieve the necessary balance, rhythm, and organization in your publication. Decide whether you want a perfectly balanced page or a more dynamic one with an off-center approach.

Establishing margins

The first principle in establishing margins is to make the bottom margin larger than the sides or top, as you usually see in framed pictures. (This looks best because the optical center of a page is actually higher than the exact center.)

Treat white space as an active element in your page design. Whether it serves the function of a place to rest the thumbs when holding the book open, or a place to rest the eyes when viewing an ad, white space is essential, and should be treated as such.

As with all rules, those about margins and white space can be broken—as long as they are understood first.

Establishing columns

Columns are basic design elements that you can use to increase readability and organize information. Columns have great aesthetic impact on any document, and should be used consistently from page to page. Columns should be separated by the correct amount of white space—too much or too little can make them look awkward. You may need to experiment with column widths and spacing before you get it right.

- If you are using a small point size, you should use narrower columns; a large point size dictates a wider column for better readability.

- Set columns on the master pages.

- Columns of equal width are not always the right design solution; for instance, a three-column page with a narrow outside column and two wider inside columns can be very versatile. Setting columns this way cannot be done automatically, however. You must set three equal columns and then adjust them by clicking on the column guides and moving them with the Pointer tool.

- Occasionally, a specific part of a page can contain different numbers of columns. This kind of arrangement still should be based on a grid, otherwise it can look haphazard and confusing.

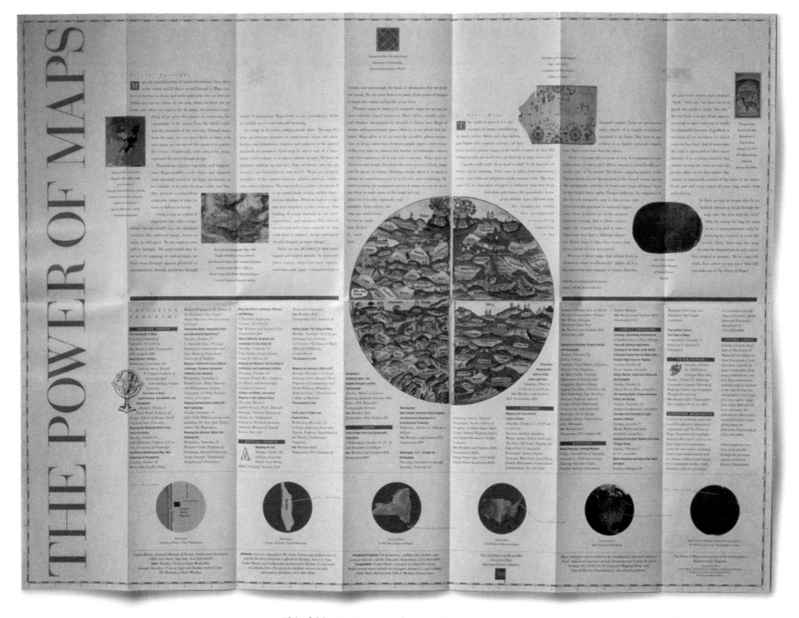

This fold-out map was designed for a museum exhibit. Notice how it makes use of different column widths: six on the top half of the page, and twelve on the bottom. Also note how photos and accompanying captions are balanced between columns—an effective way to break the monotony that repetitiveness might produce.
Designer: Christina Freyss, Pentagram Design, New York
Client: Cooper-Hewitt Museum

Build Booklet...

This function, another Aldus Addition, enables the designer of a publication to perform what is called "imposition," or structuring pages in the proper order and relationship to one another for printing back to back. It creates a copy of your publication with the pages arranged in the proper printing order. Imposition is a function that was performed traditionally by prepress professionals, and it refers to the arrangement of pages for multi-page spreads or signatures. While it can be instructive to perform this function yourself, it is a task best left to an expert—your printer. There are so many variables to consider: such as bleeds, graphics printed across two pages, registration marks, and so on, that it is risky to try and impose anything but the simplest booklet yourself. If you want to do your own imposition with Build booklet, use the Addition only when your publication is completely finished. Here is how it works:

1. Choose Build booklet from the Additions menu under the Utilities menu.

2. Select whether you want to build the booklet by first and last pages, or by the signature method of groups of 16 pages.

3. Build booklet will create a new, untitled file with the pages in the proper order, and close your original PageMaker file. Name and save the new file.

Automatic page numbering

Control-Shift-3 is the keyboard command for setting automatic page numbering. If placed on the master pages, the page numbers will appear on every page throughout the document. (This can be done on individual pages and the pages will display their correct number, if you are numbering only certain ones.) Here is how automatic page numbering works:

1. Create a text block in the correct place on the page by selecting the Text tool. Click down on the mouse button, drag the mouse and release the button before you begin typing.

2. Press the Control-Shift-3 keys. If you are on a left-hand page, you will get a text block that reads "LM"; on the right hand page, you will see "RM"; these will print as proper numbers on the succeeding pages.

3. After inserting the first automatic page number, select its text block and set the proper type specifications for font, size, style, and alignment. You also can make modifications such as typing "Page" in front of the number marker, and so forth.

4. Use the Pointer tool to ensure you have anchored the handles of the text block on the correct margins or columns.

5. If you have set the number marker for a left-hand page, and now need to do the right-hand page, copy the text block after selecting it with the Pointer tool, power paste (Control-Shift-P) it over itself by holding the Shift key to restrain it vertically, and drag the copy to the facing page. You may need to change to the Text tool, select the new number marker, and change its alignment from left aligned to right aligned, if the numbers are to be placed on the outside edge of the pages.

Sorting page order

Often it becomes necessary to change the order in which pages appear. If you are using automatic page numbering, it is extremely important that the correct page order be established and maintained.

Before this function was available as a part of the Aldus Additions, to change the order of pages it was necessary to select everything on a page, Cut it, insert a new page in the correct location, and Paste. Then you had to go back and delete the blank page. This was cumbersome, time-consuming, and risky, because it was easy to miss an item or mis-align in the paste. Now, when you have the need to change the order of pages, you simply use the Sort pages addition, and rearrange thumbnail representations of your pages. PageMaker automatically re-arranges and renumbers your pages.

In order to use the Sort pages Addition, follow these steps:

1. Choose Sort pages from the Aldus Additions menu under Utilities. A thumbnail view of your pages will appear.

2. If you are displaying facing pages in Layout view, you only can move one or more complete page spreads. If you want to sort the pages individually, click the appropriate choice in Options.

3. Select the pages you want to move—press the Shift key to select multiple pages—and drag on the pages you wish to move. Take them to their new position. If you want to change page 12/13 to become 20/21, you should drag them to the right side of 20/21 in the thumbnail view.

4. The thumbnail view will reflect both the old numbers of the pages (in dotted lines) and the new numbers after they are sorted. Click on the OK button and Sort pages does the rest. This may take some time for longer publications.

Bleeds

A bleed is a graphic, screen, or text element that extends up to the edge of the page trim. Because printing presses require a gripping edge on the paper as it is fed, ink extending all the way to the edge of the sheet will be picked up by the rollers and smeared. If you use a bleed, paper larger than the finished size must be used and trimmed when the pages dry. This generally means the printer will charge more.

Bleeds are one of the designer's most effective tools for photographs, solid colors, screens, or backgrounds. They create a sense that there is more to be seen, as if the idea being depicted is too big to be contained on a simple page.

If you intend to use a bleed, before you choose a size for your printed piece, make sure that there is a standard sheet size that will allow for the trimming. (For a list of sheet sizes, see page 51.)

When setting up the bleed in PageMaker, simply position or resize the artwork, screen, or solid color $1/4$" off the edge of the page on all sides where you want the bleed. Remember that laser printers do not print an image to the edge of the paper, so you won't see the bleed on a laser proof. High-resolution imagesetters print outside the defined page, enabling you to set up the artwork properly.

For proofing purposes, to show how the bleed will look on laser prints, reduce the percentage of the page and specify crop marks when you print. Then use a straight edge and blade to trim at the crop marks. Or, manually tile the page, specify crop marks, trim the excess, paste up the tiles by hand and trim the edges.

When using bleeds on an envelope, be aware that the printing will be done on flat sheets that will be converted to envelopes after they are printed. This will add time to a project and increase the cost. Know how long it will take to do the conversion, and what the printer will charge for doing it, before designing a bleed on an envelope.

To set up bleeds like those in the Blue Sky Design corporate identity package, follow these guidelines:

1. Set the zero point to the top right-hand corner of your page by double-clicking in the box where the rulers intersect and dragging to the corner of the page.

2. Ensure that any element measures at least $1/4$" outside on each side where it is to bleed. In the case of the blue sky—which in the actual design is a scanned photo—it must exceed the boundary of the page on the top and on the left-hand side.

3. When setting up bleeds on a document with double-sided facing pages, such as a book or brochure, remember that bleeds can be created only for the top, bottom and outside edges. To get the appearance of a bleed on an inside edge, bring your image or color exactly to the edge of the page.

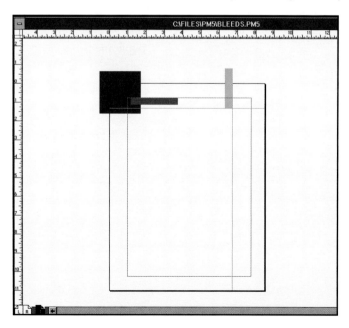

Robert Little, Joanne Little, and Maria Dominguez of Blue Sky Design in Miami created this striking corporate identity system which uses bleeds in addition to bold, primary colors.

Precise measurement is one of the most valuable capabilities of PageMaker. Even the most compulsive designer can be satisfied by the accuracy of the program. With 800% magnification, moveable zero points, Snap to guides, vertical and horizontal rules, Control palettes, and the other measuring capabilities, you won't need rulers and T-squares.

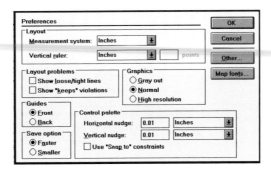

Preferences

A study of PageMaker's measurement tools should begin with Preferences under the Edit menu. Here is where you determine which measurement system to use. This menu enables you to choose whether you display guidelines in front or in back of text and graphics.

Now found under File (in earlier versions under the Edit menu), Preferences accesses functions that were designed to enable you to tailor the program to the style in which you like to work best.

■ PageMaker's Measurement system enables you to measure in inches, decimal inches, picas, millimeters, or ciceros. While each of these measurement systems has its place, most graphic artists prefer to measure in picas, partly because the measurement system is compatible with the measurement of point sizes. Some designers will use inches for a measurement system, but use picas for the vertical ruler.

■ This is where you decide whether guidelines are in front of or behind the graphics and text on the page. You can change how the guides are displayed if you have trouble grabbing them for movement.

■ Horizontal and Vertical nudge increments can be changed here for use with the Control palette.

■ Graying out detailed graphics will speed up the performance when you are doing things to the file that do not require viewing them in detail.

Rulers

Rulers are another very useful feature of PageMaker and work with flawless simplicity.

■ If rulers are not visible, you can display them by choosing Rulers from the "Guides and rulers" submenu on the Layout menu.

■ By moving the Pointer over the horizontal ruler, you can click and drag out non-printing horizontal ruler guides and check their position with the dotted lines indicated on the vertical ruler. The same is true for vertical ruler guides whose position is indicated on the horizontal ruler.

■ When you first open a publication, the zero measurements on the rulers are at the top, left-hand edge of the page. You can change this by clicking in the corner where the horizontal and vertical rulers intersect and dragging out the dotted lines. Where you release the mouse button is where you will find the new zero point measurement. This is useful for measuring specific distances between elements.

■ The Snap to rulers option is useful if you want objects positioned on exact ruler increments. Choose Snap to rulers from the Layout menu.

Guides

Guides are the backbone of PageMaker's - measurement system. Here are some of their features:

■ They can be turned on or off by choosing Guides from the Guides and rulers submenu from the Layout menu. Turning them off makes a visible difference when evaluating the aesthetics of a layout.

■ You can use the Snap to guides feature under the Guides and rulers submenu to easily align items to the guides.

■ If you have a page full of guides and want to delete them all, hold down the Shift key as you choose Guides from the Guides and rulers submenu. They will be deleted.

■ Guides can all be locked or unlocked by choosing Lock guides on the Guides and rulers submenu.

■ Common guides for all pages should be set on the master pages. Once you are on individual pages those guides can be moved. If you wish to restore them to the guides found on the master pages, choose Copy master guides from the Layout menu.

Magnification

The ability to see a magnified view of your page is very helpful when working on a small monitor, or whenever you want to see text or graphics up close.

■ The View menu under Layout will allow you to change the display from Fit in window to 400% size. You can use the commands listed, or drag and release on the size you want.

■ A useful method for changing the view is to click the right mouse button. This will toggle between Fit in window and 100% views.

■ Holding the Shift key while clicking the right mouse button toggles you between 100% and 200% views. This allows you to point the mouse to the exact location on the page you want to magnify.

■ To see an even greater magnification of any portion of your page, hold down the Control key and the spacebar, and click and drag. When you drag a small area, PageMaker will zoom to 800%.

| Fit in window | ^W |
Show pasteboard	
25% size	^0
50% size	^5
75% size	^7
Actual size	^1
200% size	^2
√ 400% size	^4

Control Palette

The Control palette offers another way to make very precise measurements. With this tool, you can manipulate text or objects with great precision by entering exact values for placement. The Control palette also enables you to make several kinds of alterations without switching to the Toolbox or choosing commands.

■ Access the Control palette by choosing it under the Windows menu, or typing Control-apostrophe. It can be moved to more convenient locations on your page by using the Pointer tool, clicking on the left-hand side bar and dragging.

■ Control palette options change depending on the object selected. Also, if you select more than one item, the control palette options will be limited to those functions that can be performed on all objects at once.

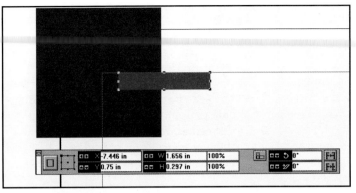

The red rectangle is selected, and the Control palette gives its location on X & Y axis, its height and width as originally drawn, and its angle of rotation (0°), and skew (0°).

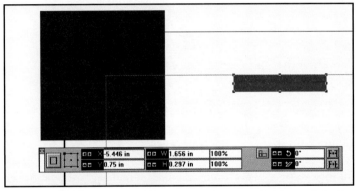

When the X axis is changed from -7.446 in. to -5.446 in. and the Enter key is pressed, the red rectangle moves two inches to the right.

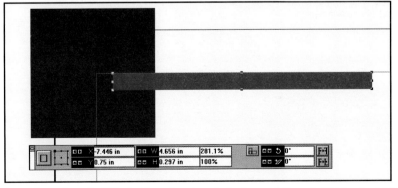

Now the value of width for the red rectangle is changed from 1.656 in. to 4.656 in. As the Enter key is pressed, the rectangle takes on the new dimensions.

■ The reference point proxy enables you to define which point on the object will be the base point for a measurement, move, rotation, skew, or reflection. You simply click on the handle in the proxy that you want to use as the reference point. In the examples here, the reference point is the center of the object.

■ To execute your transformation, once you have selected the proper measurements, click on the Apply button that appears three-dimensional when you have selected the object or press the enter key.

■ You may even use arithmetic in the numeric fields. To make a 1" box ¹/₂" wider enter +.5 after the 1 inch width and click the apply button.

■ If you want to skew or reflect an object, it can be done only with the Control palette.

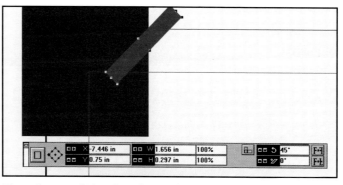

The red rectangle is selected, and rotated 45°.

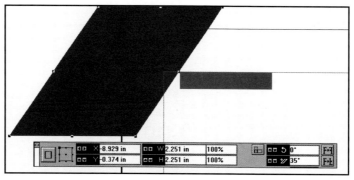

The blue rectangle is selected, and skewed 35°.

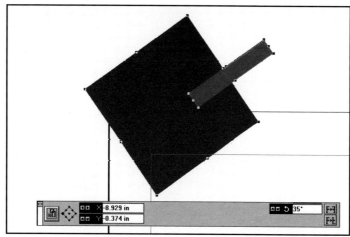

The red and blue rectangles are selected. Information about width and height is no longer displayed; together they are rotated 35°.

Formatting text with the Control Palette

The Control palette enables you to format text—either in story editor or in Layout view when using the Text tool. You can hide or display the Control palette by selecting it from the Window menu, or by typing Control-apostrophe.

There are two views available in the Control palette when formatting text: Character or Paragraph. You can toggle between these two views by clicking the Character-view or Paragraph-view button on the palette, or by typing Control-Shift-~(tilde).

- In character view, you can apply character attributes that you would normally find under the Type menu (Control-T), such as font, size, leading, and so on, to the text you have selected.

- In paragraph view, you can select alignment, styles, and other paragraph options that you would normally find under the Paragraph submenu (Control-M) to text in which you have placed the cursor.

- After selecting or clicking a text option on the Control palette, the attributes are applied to the selected text immediately. If you type a value for an option, you must apply the new setting by pressing Tab or Return, the Apply button on the left end of the palette, or by clicking another option.

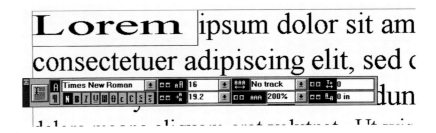

Sizing

The Pointer tool enables you to size graphics or text blocks. Using the Point tool, click on the text or graphic block to select it, point at one of the handles, and drag the mouse to make the graphic or text block larger or smaller. Holding down the Shift key when resizing imported graphics will keep them proportional. If you accidentally resize an imported graphic in only one direction, clicking on a handle while pressing the Shift key will restore its proportions—but not its original size.

Holding down the Shift key when resizing PageMaker-drawn objects will cause them to reshape to a square or a circle, depending on whether the rectangle or ellipse tool was used to draw them.

Here are some shortcuts to use when sizing:

■ If you have aligned your text block to the top guideline, use the bottom handles of the text block to narrow or widen the text block. This way, the vertical alignment of the text block will be unaffected.

■ If one side of a graphic is properly aligned, use the opposite handle for resizing— resulting in less additional measurement.

Rotation

PageMaker 5.0 has introduced free rotation for text and graphics, giving it a long-needed capability. Following these steps, it is easy to use:

1. Select the text block or graphic with the Pointer tool.

2. Change to the Rotating tool in the Toolbox and position the starburst cursor at a fixed point. (The location around which you want to rotate the object.)

3. Click and drag the cursor away from the fixed point in the direction you want to rotate the object. You will obtain more control if you drag the cursor a longer distance away, just as you would with a lever.

4. Release the mouse button when the object is in position.

5. To restrain the rotation in 45° increments, hold the Shift key down as you rotate.

After you have rotated the text, you can edit it without undoing the rotation. Simply select the text or insert the cursor with the Text tool and make the edits. If the rotation angle makes this difficult, you can switch to the Pointer tool, select the rotated text block, and open story editor (Control-E). Insert or delete text, change type, color attributes, and so forth.

Skewing or reflecting objects

By using the Control palette, it is possible to skew or reflect text or graphics.

1. Select the text block or graphic with the Pointer tool.

2. Open the Control palette either by choosing it under the Windows menu, or by typing Control-apostrophe.

3. To skew, choose a reference point from which to skew, and change the skewing value. Click the Apply button.

4. To reflect, choose a reference point from which to reflect, and click either the Horizontal-reflecting button or the Vertical-reflecting button.

Most publications are mailed and the designer must be aware of how the piece will be packaged (and how it will hold up in the mail) before initial design begins. If you are doing anything out of the ordinary, begin your design research at the post office. Ask about sizes, weights, closures, rates, and any other factors that will influence how and what you design.

Envelopes

If you intend to mail your publication in an envelope, check that there is a standard-size in a matching or coordinating paper, and that the printed piece fits well in the envelope. Don't ruin the impact of a beautifully produced publication with an envelope that's a hasty, cheap afterthought—too large (or worse, too small) for the publication inside. (See page 51 for standard envelope sizes.)

Self-mailers

If the publication is a self-mailer, consider where the name and address will go, how much postage will be required based on weight of the paper and the number of pages, and how the printed piece will hold up through handling by the post office. You may want to design a wrapper for your publication that is saddle-stitched (stapled) to it. A wrapper can be made of heavy cover stock, semi-transparent stock, or other contrasting paper and designed to be discarded, or kept as part of the piece.

Newsletters are often self-mailers. If you are creating a four-page newsletter that measures 8 1/2" x 11" before it is folded, you have the option of folding it in half or thirds for mailing. This has implications for the design:

- Don't allow headlines or photographs to be cut by folds.

- Place an interesting article on the top section of the back page. Repeat your masthead as a smaller version on the back page to immediately identify the publication.

- Determine how to close the pages for mailing. Sealing wax, string, seals, stickers, staples, or other closing devices have an impact on your design.

The newsletter below illustrates a reduced version of the nameplate from the front page for mailing purposes on the back page. This document, which was folded in thirds for mailing, had very little room to spare for mailing information, so a postcard-sized area was set up for it.
Designer: Michael J. Nolan
Client: Suzanne Clark Productions, San Francisco

Postage PAID marks

Postage marks look best if they are the same size and proportions as a normal (rather than special issue) postage stamp. Use the following steps to make them:

1. Choose the Control palette from the Windows menu.

2. Select the Rectangle tool from the Toolbox and draw a small rectangle.

3. Bring the Width and Height measurements on the Control palette to .9" x 1.2" as you draw the rectangle, or adjust the rectangle to those measurements after it is drawn.

4. Choose Fill and Line from the Element menu and select No fill and a hairline or .5 black line.

5. Create a text block within the rectangle by choosing the Type tool from the Toolbox, holding down the mouse button and dragging from the top left-hand corner of the rectangle to the bottom right-hand corner, then releasing the button.

6. Center the cursor by typing Control-Shift-C before you enter the following information: U.S. (Return) POSTAGE (Return) P A I D (Return) Permit No. (Return) XXXXXXXX (for number).

7. Change the text to a sans serif face such as Helvetica, Futura, or Avant Garde.

8. Double-click on each line and adjust the point sizes until they fit inside the rectangle. The letters should not touch the outside lines, and PAID should be much larger and bolder than the other words.

9. Change leading method to Top of Caps after choosing Spacing in the Paragraph submenu under Type. This is the easiest way to adjust the leading between individual lines. As you triple-click on each and then increase or decrease its leading, the line below responds by getting closer or farther away.

Reduced nameplates

Rather than simply typing the name of the organization sponsoring the publication, if it has a nameplate, copy and reduce that element as the identifier on the mailing page. This lends consistency and professionalism to a document. The mailing page is also a good place for the publication's masthead: who publishes it, the address, the board of directors, and similar information.

```
┌─────────────┐
│    U.S.     │
│   POSTAGE   │
│  PAID       │
│ Permit No.  │
│   456789    │
└─────────────┘
```

Signage

Don't overlook PageMaker's usefulness for making signs. Your imagination is the only limitation when it comes to creating files for output as signage.

Larger signs

If you need a sign that is larger than 8 $1/2$" x 11" and more finished looking than a laser print, consider Linotronic output—also mounted to foamcore. This creates a sign with a dense black and you can add shades of gray as well. The only drawback is that over time Linotronic output yellows, especially in the sun; but it should be serviceable for at least a year or two.

1. Check with your service bureau to see how large they can produce Linotronic output. You can create a PageMaker publication as large as 42" x 42" (if you do not use double-sided, facing pages) but its height or width should not exceed the dimensions your service bureau can output. You will be limited to a point size no larger than 650 points—which should be enough for most signage.

2. After you create your publication, send it for imagesetting, specifying that crop marks print, and then follow the procedures outlined in the section on laser printed signs for mounting and trimming. You may want to use thicker foamcore: $1/4$", $3/8$", or $1/2$".

Creating sign templates

If you want to create a template for painting a window sign, you can create your sign in PageMaker, and print it at percentage size (up to 1600% in 1% increments) that will produce the size sign you want. Use the automatic tiling feature and tape the pages together. Tape this tiled sign to the window, and trace over it on the glass. This method is also ideal for signs on cloth or other materials.

Laser printed signs

How often do you see a dog-eared 8 ½" x 11" laser print—meant to be an attractive and permanent sign—taped on the wall of a waiting area, office, or other public place? With PageMaker and a laser printer, you can make handsome, durable signs. Here is how to make signs:

1. Whether you are making just one, or a series of signs, determine a size smaller than 8 ½" x 11" so that you can print crop marks and trim the page later. This is important.

2. Set page specifications to the size you choose—also select either a tall or wide page orientation. Usually, wide is a better choice for signs. Choose margins that are equal on the top and sides, with a slightly larger bottom margin.

3. Type your information. Large, bold sans serif fonts make the best signs because they can be read from further away.

4. Print your sign(s), specifying crop marks on a high-quality laser paper. They can be black on white, black on a colored paper, or printed solid black with reverse type.

5. Using a spray fixative, mount the sign(s) to a piece of ⅛" foamcore.

6. Using a sharp blade and a straight edge, trim the sign at the crop marks.

7. Spray the sign with artist's fixative—which will protect it—darken the black and make it slightly shiny.

8. Mount the sign with double-sided tape.

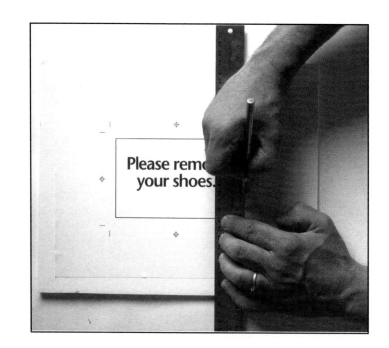

The advent of personal computers and the introduction of programs like Aldus PageMaker greatly impacted the centuries-old art of typography. Quality type does not just happen. To become a PageMaker expert, you must develop a basic understanding of typography, which you can gain from careful study and observation of the typographic world around us.

Fonts are the basis of any PageMaker design. Choosing the best typefaces for the job is the beginning. Making them work best is an art.

serif

sans serif

Choosing serif or sans serif

Conventional wisdom holds that you read serif typefaces (such as Times Roman, Bodoni, or Palatino) easier than sans serif faces (Helvetica, Futura, Franklin Gothic). When readability is important, use serif faces for body copy. This is because you read text from left to right. The eye scans a group of words, pauses, and then moves on to the next group. The horizontal serifs on the mostly vertical letterforms direct the eye along the horizontal axis.

Sans serif typefaces convey an air of directness with their uncluttered, simple forms. For this reason, they are a good choice for headlines or display text; they impart an immediacy to any message. Because some sans serif faces are very heavy, they read well from a great distance. They also work well when printed in color.

Although the rules for using serif and sans serif faces for body copy and headlines are not steadfast, if you want to break a rule, it's probably better to set headlines in a serif font than to set body text in a sans serif font.

It is seldom advisable to combine two serif or two sans serif fonts in the same document, unless they have markedly different characteristics such as weight, width, or size.

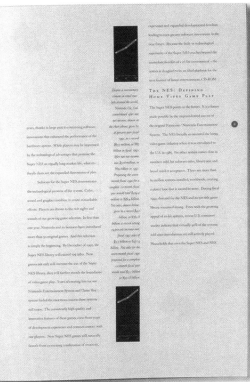

This annual report design succeeds in part because of its typographical sophistication. Balance, color, variety, and white space work together to create impact.
Designer: Dorothy A. Cross,
Leimer Cross Design, Seattle
Client: Nintendo Co., Ltd.

Assessing your fonts

Before you begin your design, determine what fonts you have available and how you can work with them most effectively. Most PostScript laser printers come with a set of basic fonts—usually Avant Garde, Bookman, Courier, Helvetica, Helvetica Narrow, New Century Schoolbook, Palatino, Symbol, Times, Zapf Chancery, and Zapf Dingbats.

If you are limited to a laser printer's basic fonts, you still can create beautiful documents by paying attention to good typography. The list below suggests uses for the basic fonts.

■ Avant Garde

This font can be quite decorative for signage and headlines, but may be a poor choice for body text. Based on the circle, its letterforms have an open, airy feeling. Avant Garde is a good font to condense or extend.

AVANT GARDE:
Cool and aloof.

■ Bookman

Bookman bold is ideal for headlines and can be used for body text in its lighter version. It has a friendly, informal feeling. Because of its wide characters, it is not very economical for getting a lot of copy into a small space.

Bookman is warm
and friendly.

If you want your publication to look like it was typewritten, **Courier** is the right choice.

■ Courier

Use Courier when you want your publication to look like it was created on a typewriter. Because Courier does not have proportional spacing, each character takes up the same amount of space—whether it is a W or an I.

■ Helvetica

Based on a design originally created for London Underground signage in the 1800s, Helvetica gained popularity in the 1950s for its balance and purity of form. After its introduction, it became very popular—almost too much so. It is sometimes used without much thought simply because it is considered a safe choice.

Helvetica makes good signage and headlines—especially its bold version. Generally, it is not a good choice for body text.

HELVETICA:
Classic form.

■ Helvetica-Narrow

Many laser printers come with the HelveticaNarrow font. It is not recommended for body text because it is difficult to read, but it makes great headlines when it is set in a large point size.

Originally, Helvetica-Narrow had no high-resolution equivalent for Linotronic output. This caused great confusion when it was used in place of Condensed Helvetica. When files were sent for imagesetting, the font could not be printed because it is not possible to convert Helvetica-Narrow to Helvetica Condensed.

Look Sally! See Spot.
New Century makes it
easy to read.

■ New Century Schoolbook

An overlooked gem, New Century Schoolbook, is a face with beautiful impact when used as display type. At the same time, it can be very effective as body text. Its school book origin makes the reader feel comfortable instantly and its straightforward simplicity makes it ideal for books and manuals.

Watch the beautiful Palatino Italic "dance" across a page.

■ **Palatino**

Palatino was modeled from type found carved in stone in Roman ruins. Its classical elegance conveys an air of conservatism, solidity, and grace. (Think of publications for banks, churches, or foundations.)

Palatino has a beautiful italic face—one that dances across a page. This italic is an appropriate choice for lead-ins, pull quotes, or captions.

■ **Symbol**

Use Symbol for mathematical equations and technical documents.

$$\alpha\,\beta\,\chi\,\delta\,\varepsilon\,\phi\,\gamma\,\varphi\,o\,\kappa\,\lambda$$
$$\mu\,\pi\,[\,\theta\,\rho\,\sigma\,\tau\,\iota\,\varpi\,\omega\,\xi\,\upsilon\,\zeta$$

■ **Times**

Derived from a design originated by *The London Times* (circa 1850), to get the most legible text into the smallest amount of space, Times succeeds today as a versatile face. It combines formal elegance with business-like conviction. Times is an excellent choice for body text because of its economy. It also makes a particularly beautiful display face—conveying an image of strength, order, and clarity.

■ **Zapf Chancery**

Script fonts have a calligraphic or handwritten feeling. They give a feeling of elegance and ease. Zapf Chancery, the only script font in the basic laser printer group, is good for invitations and other informal uses. In a large point size, it makes interesting initial caps. When skewed or stretched, its calligraphic forms are emphasized. This font is extremely

See how dramatic Zapf Chancery can be when it's skewed and rotated?

■ **Zapf Dingbats**

This type provides emphasis to a statement or a decorative treatment. However, dingbats must be used with care: too many on a page create a cluttered look.

If you are uncertain where to find a particular Zapf Dingbat select Character Map from the Accessories group. It works like this:

1. In Character Map, select Zapf Dingbats from the font drop down box.

2. All of the characters available in the Zapf Dingbats font appear in the Character Map screen. Click and hold the mouse on the character to see a magnified view of that character. The key combination required to enter that character is shown in the extreme lower right corner of the character map screen. Please note that the number should be entered on your keyboard's numeric keypad.

3. You also can select a character and copy it through the Clipboard.

hard to read in all caps.

Times isn't often considered for headlines, but it makes good ones.

Adding fonts

Most professional designers buy additional fonts—and there are numerous ones from which to choose. Your personal preferences will determine what you buy. Font packages range in price from a few dollars to two or three hundred dollars each. Before you purchase a font, make sure that your service bureau can output that font.

Downloaded fonts

Fonts that you purchase and add to your system must be downloaded to your printer—hence the name. This is not a difficult technical maneuver (refer to your documentation). What is more difficult is choosing from the thousands of fonts available.

Here are some personal favorites you may consider when building a foundation for your font library:

■ **Serif**
  Bodoni, Cheltenham, Garamond, Garamond Condensed, Goudy, New Baskerville

■ **Sans Serif**
  Futura, Futura Condensed, Helvetica Black, Helvetica Compressed, Helvetica Condensed, Univers, Franklin Gothic

■ **Script**
  Shelley, Brush Script, Park Avenue

■ **Other**
  Sumner Stone's Adobe font, Stone provides serif, sans serif, and informal faces—all of which you can use together effectively. (This book is set in Stone.)

Some sources for fonts

Adobe Systems
(800) 83-FONTS

Agfa
(800) 424-8973

Autologic
(800) 457-8973

Bitstream
(800) 237-3553

Casady & Greene
(408) 484-9228

Digital Typeface Corporation
(612) 944-9264

Emigre
(800) 944-9021

The Font Company
(602) 998-9711

FontHaus, Inc.
(800) 942-9110

Fonts West
(415) 777-3011

ImageClub Graphics
(403) 262-8008

International Typeface Corp. (ITC)
(212) 371-0699

Letraset
(800) 343-TYPE

Linotype
(800) 633-1900

Monotype
(800) MONOTYPE

NEC Technologies
(800) 826-2255

TYPE

75

Choosing the right typeface and its specifications are critical design decisions. Remember that readability comes first. Choose point sizes, weight, leading, line length, alignment, colors, and other attributes with care.

Text alignment

PageMaker's text handling capabilities allow for left aligned, centered, right aligned, justified, and force justified text. There are rules for choosing these options, too.

■ Left aligned

The most readable choice for body text is left aligned. Its consistent word spacing and varying rag along the right-hand side make it easier for the eye to track from the end of one line to the beginning of the next. Left-aligned text combines a no-nonsense look with modern informality, yielding a sensible, straightforward feeling.

Centered text can

be more effective

when it's emphasized,

given lots of attention,

and space.

■ Centered

Centered text is more formal. Use it for headlines, pull-quotes, and other display situations. In PageMaker, be careful where you locate the text block handles—or the text may be centered within its block, not the column or the page. Also, avoid using indents and tabs when centering text; they may throw off lines in relation to one another.

Dear friend of Visiting Nurse Service:
The process of preparing an annual report to our membership is often profoundly educational. In reflecting on where we've come from, we see more clearly in which directions we must head. ¶ What can we learn from 1991? Overwhelmingly, the lessons center on growth - both internally and in the needs of the community we serve. ¶ The data that you will read in the following pages tells the story of a burgeoning client population with a need for more and more sophisticated home care technology. 1991 saw a 30% increase in total home visits and a 35% increase in skilled nursing visits. While these numbers reflect that many patients now require more frequent home care visits, they also reflect a 33% increase in the total number of patients served. This growth takes on more significance when you consider the competition in the market for home health care. At the beginning of 1991, there were 36 such agencies in our service area. By the end of the year, there were 46. ¶ In 1991, VNS continued to face the challenges of a diminishing supply of skilled employees. Our staff grew by 19%, but viewed against a patient load that grew three times as much, the picture is one of employees often stretched to their limits. The challenge is to support these employees with the technology that can help them be more effective under these conditions. For example, in 1991 we dedicated $150,000 to the upgrade of the computer systems that most of our employees depend on to ease their administrative load. ¶ Among the most important areas of growth was an increase in our fund balance for 1991. We reported an operating deficit of 190,752 in 1990. After a review of Medicare

reimbursement for 1990 based on a new Discrete Costing Methodology, a settlement with Blue Cross of Illinois (fiscal intermediary for Medicare) resulted in an operating surplus of around $425,674 in 1991. Half of this can be attributed to the 1990 cost report settlement. ¶ As the needs of those we serve seemed to increase exponentially throughout 1991, the VNS Board of Directors sought to create a foundation for internal growth to support the resulting challenges to our organization. The entire board spent a period of time in study of the legal and ethical implications surrounding employees with AIDS. We submitted a successful appeal to the United Way for $50,000 in additional projected funding for 1992. We also began the process of self-study and evaluation required periodically of United Way-funded organizations and made application for national accreditation to the Joint Commission on Accreditation of Health Organizations. ¶ The growth that characterized 1991 puts VNS in a position of tremendous opportunity – and responsibility – as we answer the call to find better and more effective ways to serve our clients. New programs reflected a renewed focus on family, a rededication to our belief that if we pay as much attention to what surrounds our clients as to the disease process taking place inside, healing will be swifter, more effective and more complete. We continued to explore technological advances so that we can respond to the increasing acuity level of our clients' health concerns. But more important, we continued to research better ways to put our skills to work in the treatment of not just the disease but the whole person. ¶ We appreciate the opportunity to bring you up to date on the fascinating changes VNS faced in 1991, and we look forward to sharing how we progress in 1992.

Sincerely,

Spencer M. Vawter
Chairman of the Board

Harriett H. Olson
President and CEO

The brochure at the left illustrates deliberate and effective use of type alignment. The arrangement follows a subtle step theme used throughout the publication.
Designers: Laura Lacy-Sholly & James Sholly
Antenna, Indianapolis
Client: The Visiting Nurse Association

■ Right aligned

Because right-aligned text is contrary to how we read, use it very sparingly. It works in special applications such as captions on the left of a photo or illustration, or as a large-size introductory phrase or paragraph at the beginning of an article.

Right aligned text makes an interesting lead-in to a paragraph of body text if it's treated like this.

■ Justified

This text treatment is formal, yet commonplace in magazines and newspapers. It brings strict order to a page. If you choose it for body copy, handle it carefully. Justifying text is more tricky than most people realize. Unless you achieve the right balance between point size and column width, you may end up with too few words on a line, creating exaggerated spaces between words. Justified text also requires that you pay close attention to hyphenation. Too many lines ending with hyphens is tiresome and jarring: too few hyphenated words will create uneven word spacing.

Lorem ipsum dolor sit amet, consectetuer adipiscing elit, sed diam nonummy nibh euismod tincidunt ut laoreet dolore magna aliquam erat volutpat. Ut wisi enim ad minim veniam, quis nostrud exerci tation ullamcorper suscipit lobortis nisl ut aliquip ex ea commodo consequat. Duis autem vel eum iriure dolor in hendrer.

This column is too narrow for justified type   this size; as a result, it looks a w k w a r d and unbalanced.

■ Force justified

Force justified text is like justified, except that the last line of a paragraph is justified—even if it contains only a few characters. When used with words of similar length, it can give a stylish appearance. Often, it can create a hard to read, self-conscious design. Use sparingly.

FORCE   JUSTIFIED   TEXT
CAN   BE   VERY   STYLISH

Point sizes and column widths

Point size should relate to column width. If point size is too large, words cannot form enough groups on a short line that the eye needs for efficient reading. If line lengths are too long and filled with small type, the eye can lose its place reading from the end of one line to the beginning of the next. Generally, your column is too narrow if it contains fewer than 8 words; more than 20 words may result in a column that it is too wide. Once again, this isn't a steadfast rule, rather a rule of thumb made to be broken if the situation warrants.

This column is too wide for type this small, unless it's for some kind of contract where you want to make the fine print hard to read. If there are many justified lines of this length, it is easy for the reader to get lost when scanning from the end of one line to the beginning of the next.

Font styles

Most fonts contain a bold, italic, and bold italic version. Some, such as Avant Garde shown on the right, have even more weights. Together these versions make up a font family. The font designer created each version with its own defining characteristics. When using PageMaker, you can access the bold and italic variations of a font by selecting Bold or Italic in the Type Specs dialog box. If these variations do not exist in the font you have selected, Pagemaker will create a simulation of the bold or italic effect. These fattened or obliqued versions of the original face are not the true bold or italic. As clumsy as it may seem, you should select the proper font, (e.g., B Garamond Bold), rather than simply checking Bold in a dialog box.

Avant Garde Extra Light
Extra Light Oblique
Avant Garde Book
Book Oblique
Avant Garde Medium
Medium Oblique
Avant Garde Demi
Demi Oblique
Avant Garde Bold
Bold Oblique

Bodoni Regular
Bodoni Italic
Bodoni Bold
Bodoni Bold Italic

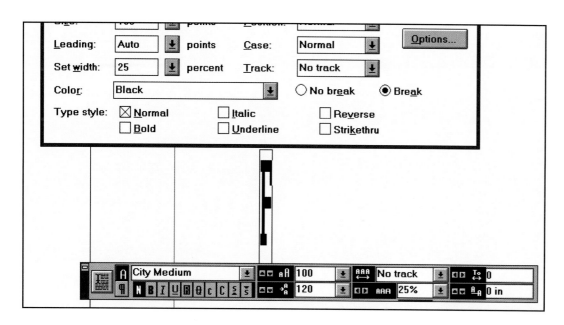

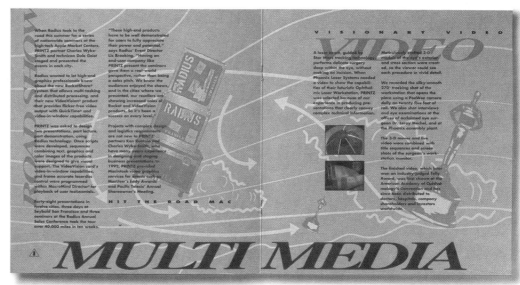

Transforming type

One of the most exciting features PageMaker offers the designer is the power to transform type. It is simple to expand or compress type, providing opportunities for abstraction and looking at the conventional in fresh ways. This power also carries the potential to create distortions of carefully configured letterforms, and many design and typography purists object to it. In spite of that, transformed type has become a hallmark of electronic publishing design.

You can transform type by going into the Type specs menu and altering Set width to a different percentage size. (The default is 100%.) You also can use the Control palette for this function. The F in the figure above has been compressed to 25 percent of its normal width.

This brochure's type was expanded to 120% to emphasize the electronic production capabilities of the company.
Designer: Mike Bertoni
Client: PRINTZ Electronic Design

Reverses

Sometimes the eye seeks something different. The term "reverse" denotes a total opposite in terms of color—from positive to negative. Like anything else, reversed type can be very effective if it is done well. Here are some guidelines to follow:

- Be careful not to use a typeface with thin letter strokes. These can fill in when printed because of dot gain or other ink coverage problems.

- Avoid using small point sizes unless the typeface is really bold.

- You can use reversed type as visual dividers to indicate a section or subsection of a publication.

- Carefully consider the framing for your reversed type. Keep an adequate border of solid color around the type. Also note how the solid background works in the context of the entire page. Is it more dominant than the type inside it? Should it be?

- In books (such as this one) reverses can double as thumb tabs when they bleed off the edge of the page.

Creating reverses as a style

If your publication has many instances that call for the same treatment of information in a reverse bar, define a Paragraph style by following the steps below. You will save time and achieve perfect measurement where you apply the style.

1. Type a word or phrase. Make certain its type specifications are correct and that the text block is the proper width. Choose Reverse to set the color to paper.

2. Use the Text tool to select the text; choose Paragraph from the Type menu and select Rules.

3. Choose a rule thickness at least as big as the text point size. Decide if you want the rules to be the width of the text or the width of the column. (Width of column is probably better because it provides consistency in repetitive visual elements on the page.) Choose a color for rules if you are printing in color.

4. Select Options and alter the measurements for the rules above and below the baseline. You may need to view the adjustments a few times before you get the measurement just right.

5. With the entire line selected, using the Text tool, choose Define styles from the Text menu. While your selection is highlighted, click on New. Name the style and click on the OK button to confirm your choice. (After the new style appears in the style palette, select your original text and apply that style to it.) You now have created a style that you can apply throughout your publication with ease.

Tuesday, March 6

Lorem Ipsum dolor sit amet, consectetuer adipiscing elit, sed diam nonummy nibh euismod tincidunt ut laoreet dolore quam erat volutpat. Ut n ad minim veniam, strud exerci tation per suscipit lobortis iquip ex ea commodo t.

Styles

[No style]
Body text
Caption
Hanging indent
Headline
Subhead 1
Subhead 2

Wednesday, March 7

Duis autem vel eum iriure dolor in hendrerit in vulputate velit esse molestie consequat, vel illum dolore eu feugiat nulla facilisis at vero eros et accumsan et iusto odio dignissim qui blandit praesent luptatum zzril delenit augue duis dolore te feugait nulla facilisi.

All caps and small caps

Setting type in all caps can create emphasis. However, if you use all caps (even for a headline) you can make it harder to read your message—not easier. This is because the variation found in upper and lower case letters helps the eye track across the text. In most instances, using all caps for body text is inappropriate.

Small caps will substitute upper case letters for those that normally would be lower case, (in a smaller point size than the letters would be if they were capitalized.) When used for small amounts of text, such as headlines or pull quotes, small caps can add a refined look to a publication. If used as body text, small caps look contrived and are hard to read.

Applying colors to type

You can print type in spot color or in process colors. If you wish to assign a color to letters or words, simply use the Text tool from the Toolbox, select the desired text, and choose the color from the color palette. (See page 34 for a discussion of spot vs. process color.)

Use color type carefully. Headlines in a second color usually carry less emphasis than they do in full black. Body text becomes more difficult to read. Pull quotes, drop caps, and similar lead-ins are appropriate candidates for colorizing.

LOREM IPSUM DOLOR SIT AMET, CONSECTETUER ADIPISCING ELIT, SED DIAM NONUMMY NIBH EUISMOD TINCIDUNT UT LAOREET DOLORE MAGNA ALIQUAM ERAT VOLUTPAT. UT WISI ENIM AD MINIM VENIAM, QUIS NOSTRUD EXERCI TATION ULLAMCORPER SUSCIPIT

Notice the difference between type set in all caps on the left, and small caps on the right. Both text blocks contain the same words, set in the same point size.

LOREM IPSUM DOLOR SIT AMET, CONSECTETUER ADIPISCING ELIT, SED DIAM NONUMMY NIBH EUISMOD TINCIDUNT UT LAOREET DOLORE MAGNA ALIQUAM ERAT VOLUTPAT. UT WISI ENIM AD MINIM VENIAM, QUIS NOSTRUD EXERCI TATION ULLAMCORPER SUSCIPIT

The Type specs... menu

When I first saw this menu in PageMaker 1.0A, I fell in love then and there with the program. Realizing the potential to easily change the characteristics of all the text in a document, I learned quickly that Control-T can bring nearly instant gratification.

The first six functions under the Type menu also are found under the Type specs... pop-up menu. This menu offers a pull-down shortcut when you want to change a single characteristic of type, such as its font, size, etc.

Font	▶
Size	▶
Leading	▶
Set width	▶
Track	▶
Type style	▶
Type specs...	^T
Paragraph...	^M
Indents/tabs...	^I
Hyphenation...	^H
Alignment	▶
Style	▶
Define styles...	^3

The Type pull-down menu is where you access Type specifications. Type specs... contains the first six choices in the Type menu and others not shown here.

The full Type specifications menu is much more than just a place to change a font or point size. Let's look at some of its features:

■ **Font**

This is where you select the proper font for your text. Using the Text tool, you must select your text first to change the font of text already placed.

■ **Size**

In PageMaker, you can specify type sizes from 4 to 650 points. Clicking on the arrow to the right of the Size box, you can quickly choose preset sizes for selected text. However, if you wish to assign a size not on the list, (such as 33 point), or sizes in $^1/_{10}$ point increments, you will need to enter a specific number in the dialog box.

■ **Leading**

Leading refers to the space between lines of text. In PageMaker, it is measured in point sizes from 0 to 1600. There are three ways you can set leading: Proportional, Top of caps, and Baseline. These methods are explained on page 85.

■ **Set width**

This is one way to expand or compress type. Specify a set percentage already found on the pull-down menu, or type in your own value. You can make type as wide as 250% of the normal value, or as narrow as 5%. Remember, changing the width affects the type's readability and purity of form, and if applied to large amounts of type, will significantly slow down screen refreshes of that text.

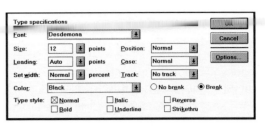

The Type specifications menu dialog box.

■ **Color**

This little menu serves the same function as the Color palette. Determining your type's color while choosing other type specifications is very convenient. Clicking on the Color box and dragging down reveals your choices.

■ **Type style**

Click Italic, Bold, Underline, etc. to change type style. If you select a bold font, such as B Garamond Bold, do not assign the bold attribute to it in the Type specifications box. Likewise, do not choose italic this way for a font such as Goudy Italic.

■ **Position**

Normal, superscript, and subscript are the three choices under position. Superscript reduces the size of the character, and places it above the baseline, as for a footnote reference number. Subscript reduces the size and places the character below the baseline. The easiest way to use the position function is to type the entire line of text and then select the individual letters you want to superscript or subscript.

Case

It's very easy to select a block of text, open Type specs... and choose the All caps option. Be aware that if you key in the text using the Caps Lock key, you cannot go back and automatically change that text to upper and lower case. For that reason, it is good practice to key in text as upper and lower case. Small caps is the other option under Case, other than Normal.

Track

Tracking controls how loose or tight individual letters are in relation to one another. Under Track you can choose No track, Very loose, Loose, Normal, Tight, and Very tight tracking. Tracking affects larger point sizes more than it does smaller ones. When you apply tracking to type, you should run laser proofs until you are happy with how the type looks. Tracking can have a very dramatic impact.

Options

Options under the Type specs... menu provide PageMaker users with more specificity in determining percentages for the size of small caps in relation to point size, superscript and subscript sizes and positions, and baseline shift. Baseline shift enables you to specify individual words or letters in a line and shift their position— relative to the baseline—either up or down by specific increments.

Paragraph specifications

The Paragraph menu, found in the Type pull-down menu, can set indents and alignment, but you can find those functions easily elsewhere. I find its greatest use is in creating extra space between paragraphs. Using global functions such as paragraph styles in conjunction with features like extra paragraph spacing give documents the consistency that marks professional work.

Adding space between paragraphs

Using this option, you do not need to insert extra carriage returns between paragraphs. You also can ensure that headlines or subheads are always followed by the correct amount of spacing before body text begins. To add extra space before or after a paragraph, follow these steps:

1. Place your cursor in a paragraph and access the Paragraph submenu from the Type menu, or type Control-M.

2. It's most useful to use points and picas for measurement. In the dialog box under Paragraph space, type the desired amount of space in picas. You can use points too. Remember, 6 picas equals one inch; there are twelve points to a pica. Therefore, 1p6 would mean 1 pica and 6 points, or 1 1/2 picas. These points are the same points used to measure type, so if you are using 10 point type on 12 point leading, one pica (12 points) between paragraphs would be the same space as one carriage return.

3. Click on the OK button. Now, each time you type a return to end one paragraph and begin a new one, the new one will begin the correct distance away from the preceding paragraph.

Breaking paragraphs

Another useful function of the Paragraph submenu is its capability to control where paragraphs break. You can specify that lines stay together, begin a column, or begin a new page. Widow and orphan controls determine the minimum number of lines in a paragraph that are allowed to end or begin columns of text. (One line is never acceptable for a widow or orphan. It may take at least three lines to avoid the widow-orphan look.)

Paragraph rules

You also can create paragraph styles that have rules above and below text; and, rules that have specific weights, colors, and vertical distances away from text blocks. You can even create rules thick enough to lay under the text. (See page 80, "Creating reverses as a style" for a description of how paragraph rules work.)

Letter, word, line, and paragraph spacing are all very important design considerations. An understanding of how spacing works will help you achieve greater control working with type.

▪ Letter spacing by kerning

In PageMaker you can adjust the space between letters, kerning manually or automatically under the Spacing attributes menu. Kerning type means increasing or decreasing the space between characters to achieve a more even fit between pairs of letters. To kern, PageMaker measures each letter's distance from the letter preceding it as a percentage of the word space (the distance entered when you press the space bar, known as an em space).

Manually kern letters by placing the cursor between two characters and using the following key combinations:

- To increase spacing 1/25 em space, press the Control key and the right cursor arrow.
- To increase spacing 1/100 em space, press the Shift key and the Control-right cursor arrow.
- To decrease spacing 1/25 em space, press the Control key and the left cursor arrow.
- To decrease spacing 1/100 em space, press the Shift key, the Control key, and the left cursor arrow.

You can apply Automatic pair kerning at the paragraph level. This will change every kern pair in an entire paragraph. With a paragraph selected, or as you define a paragraph style, check Automatic pair kerning in the Paragraph specifications dialog box under the Type menu.

Sometimes it is desirable to use Page-Maker's default kerning, particularly if you cannot remember what manual kerning you have applied to a word, or group of words. You can do this by selecting a range of text and entering 0 for the kerning percentage on the Control palette, or by pressing Shift-Control-0 (zero).

WAVE
7.
1994

WAVE
7.
1994

In the examples above, the red type illustrates typical kerning problems. The blue type shows improved kerning by tightening the spaces between certain characters.

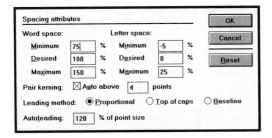

The Spacing attributes menu is a submenu of the Paragraph menu (Control-M).

■ Letter spacing by tracking

Tracking is a global adjustment that moves all the letters in a text block closer together or farther apart.

You can find the Track feature under the Type specs submenu where you can choose five different degrees of tracking: from Very loose to Very tight. This is found under the Track command on the Type menu.

■ Word spacing

While it is possible to change word spacing in the Spacing submenu, doing so deviates from the font designer's ideal spacing. There is little reason for changing word spacing unless you're trying to clean up a text block by bringing up a single word from another line, or you want to reduce hyphenation in justified text. In either case, you must enter a value for minimum that is less than that desired, and a value for maximum that is greater than that desired.

■ Line spacing

Line spacing can be a very effective design tool. It imparts a rhythm to a page. You can control Line spacing through the Leading feature in the Type specs submenu.

■ Leading

Leading is the technical term for line spacing. Increased leading creates more space between lines; decreased leading creates less space between lines. In PageMaker there are three settings for positioning text within its leading (see illustration below). You can find them by choosing Paragraph under the Type menu, and clicking on the Spacing button.

Duis autem vel eum iriure dolor in hendrerit in vulputate.

Proportional leading is the default leading setting and places the baseline of the text two-thirds of the way down from the top of the slug.

Duis autem vel eum iriure dolor in hendrerit in vulputate.

Top-of-caps leading measures the distance from the highest point of the tallest character in the line—regardless of the type's point size.

Duis autem vel eum iriure dolor in hendrerit in vulputate.

Baseline leading aligns the bottom of the slug with the baseline of a line of text.

There are reasons for using each of the three leading methods. If you have different type point sizes in a paragraph, you may want to choose Proportional leading. If you want to align text to a grid, Baseline (the method used in traditional typography) is helpful. Use Top-of-caps to adjust leading line by line when each line of text is a different point size.

■ Spacing between sentences

Many typists and word processors instinctively place two spaces between sentences. This is contrary to typesetting conventions that call for only one space. (Otherwise, you invite "rivers" of white space flowing down your columns.) You can use the Change command under Story editor, to search and replace double spaces with single spaces. Even if you input the text yourself, it is always possible that you may have entered two spaces here or there. You'll be happier finding them before you output your files than after your document is printed.

PageMaker can place text in your publication from many different sources including Windows word processing files and text files from other platforms. Correctly importing text is very important in the production process.

Typewritten or printed text

If the copy for your design comes from type-written or printed pages, instead of an electronic file—you can have the pages scanned using an Optical Character Recognition (OCR) software program and a scanner to save time. Once scanned, the text can be saved in a common word-processing format and then edited in PageMaker. Although these programs can be difficult to use, many service bureaus can do the scanning for you. This is a good solution if there is a large amount of text to enter.

Text from word processing programs

PageMaker can import text from numerous word processing programs—including Microsoft Word, Microsoft Works, WordPerfect, XyWrite, and others, from both Macintosh and PC platforms.

There are many ways to get text from a Mac into PageMaker on your PC. Most Macintosh computers shipped since the release of the SE-30, include a disk drive that can read and write 3.5" floppy disks using a program called Apple File Exchange. There is also conversion hardware (such as disk drives from Dayna) and software (such as MacLink). You also can send text files over a modem from a Macintosh to a PC, in which case you will need to use ASCII, or the text only format. Transferring files using the ASCII format results in losing the majority of the file's formatting.

Style sheet characteristics

If you can retain the file's formatting when converting a PC word processing file or importing a Macintosh file, styling characteristics such as character (bold, italic), paragraph (spacing, indents), and style attributes (font, point size, leading) will be imported into the PageMaker document and will not need to be reapplied.

When PageMaker imports style characteristics from a word processing program, it adds the style to your publication's style palette with an asterisk (*) next to the style's name. If you already have a style by that name in your PageMaker document, the text will be formatted in the PageMaker style and the asterisk does not appear.

Style-name tags

When preparing text in a text only, or ASCII word-processing program, you can add style-name tags at the beginning of each paragraph that you import into PageMaker and want interpreted as a style. This means that text created with a word processing program can be assigned styles, even if the program does not support paragraph style definitions. The designations look like this: <headline>, <body text>, etcetera. Place the tags at the beginning of each paragraph that requires a change in style. There can be no characters or spaces preceding them. A tag that contains no name (< >) will be treated as if it has no assigned style.

PageMaker will apply the style to the paragraph that follows the tag and to all subsequent paragraphs, until it finds a different style-name tag.

When importing documents with style-name tags, use Place under the File menu, and check the Read tags option. The style-name tag must match a style already defined in the PageMaker file before importing the text.

From database/spreadsheet programs

Spreadsheet files created in Excel and Lotus 1-2-3 formats can be imported as text into PageMaker. When you import text from a database or spreadsheet program, it may require extensive formatting in PageMaker because style attributes from the original program are sometimes lost.

You generally will want to export spreadsheets as tab delimited text, (which means that a tab will be inserted between the data in each cell). This makes formatting the data using the Indents/tabs feature in PageMaker easier.

For specific information about how to export spreadsheet and database files as text, refer to the manuals for those programs.

From other PageMaker publications

When importing text from one PageMaker 5.0 file into another, open both files, click on the text block you want to copy with the Pointer tool, and drag it to the new file. This will copy the text displayed in the first file into the new one.

Other times, you can open one PageMaker file, select all the text in one story by placing the Text tool cursor in the text block, select all (Control-A) and copy (Control-C). When you open the new file, select the Text tool, click the cursor on the page and paste (Control-V). The text retains its specifications.

If you need to place numerous stories that are in separate text blocks from different pages from one PageMaker file to another, you can use the Story import filter. Use the following steps:

1. Open a new publication.

2. Choose Place from the File menu (Control-D).

3. Locate the publication from which to import text stories. Click on the OK button.

4. The Story import dialog box will display. It shows the first several characters of each story.

5. Shift-click the stories you want and click on the OK button.

6. You will get the loaded place icon. Click on the page where you want to place the text.

TYPE

87

Headlines are important in the design of any publication. Although headlines may vary from article to article, they provide an underlying consistency in your design. Usually, headlines contrast with body text in size, color, weight, font choice, or placement.

The headline, "We Have to Change Congress," is the focal point of this campaign brochure.
Designer: Michael J. Nolan
Client: Joe Nation for Congress Committee

Headline uses

Headlines grab attention. They must be well-written, succinct, and easy to read. The amount of contrast between the headline and the body text is an important design decision.

You can achieve contrast using different techniques: color, font selection, point size, weight, or placement. Choose one or two techniques and apply them consistently throughout your publication.

- Use a color headline above black body text.

- Use a different, much bolder font in the same or even smaller point size.

- Use a different point size featuring a larger, but lighter face for the headline.

- Span all the columns of an article with its headline.

- Indent or outdent the headline.

- Rotate the headline, or insert it into the body text.

- Use stepping down type—a very old technique—that can lead from headline to body text.

Bolder, 1 point smaller &different font
Lorem ipsum dolor sit amet, consectetuer adipiscing elit, sed diam non ummy nibh euismod tincidunt. Ut laoreet dolore magna aliquam erat volutpat.

Lighter font, larger point size, another color.

Ut wisi enim ad minim veniam, quis nostrud exerci. Tation ullamcorper suscipit lobortis nisl ut aliquip ex ea commodo consequat. Hendrerit in vulputate velit esse molestie consequat, vel illum dolore eu feugiat nulla facilisis at vero eros et accumsan et iusto odio dignissim qui blandit praesent luptatum zzril delenit augue duis dolore te feugait nulla facilisi.

This is an example of the very old, but very useful, stepping-down type technique.

Duis autem vel eum iriure dolor in hendrerit in vulputate velit esse molestie consequat, vel illum dolore eu feugiat nulla facilisis at vero eros et accumsan et iusto odio dignissim qui blandit praesent luptatum zzril delenit augue duis dolore te feugait nulla facilisi. Nam liber tempor cum soluta nobis eleifend option congue nihil imperdiet doming id quod mazim placerat facer possim assum.

An Outdented Headline Works Well

Dolor sit amet, consectetuer adipiscing elit, sed diam non ummy nibh euismod tincidunt ut laoreet dolore magna aliquam erat volutpat. Ut wisi enim ad minim veniam, quis nostrud exerci tation ullamcorper suscipit lobortis nisl ut aliquip ex ea commodo consequat.

Headline guidelines

There are many ways to ensure the best use of headlines:

- Limit the number of headline treatments and ensure that you apply the treatments consistently by using style definitions.

- Coordinate headlines with subheads by deriving subheads from either headline or body text fonts.

- Avoid all caps in headlines; they can be hard to read. Writers often use all caps for headlines as they type. You may need to rekey headline text if heads are in all caps.

- Avoid the underline type style. If you set underlined words in headlines, they look clunky and are hard to read, thereby giving the headline less emphasis. If you must underline, use paragraph rules or the Line tool in PageMaker and control the weight, color, and placement of the underscoring.

- Don't use too many fonts, sizes, or colors. If you treat every headline differently, the reader cannot establish a visual hierarchy to determine the most important articles. The publication takes on a messy, jumbled appearance.

- Be careful how you handle rules and other column conventions. If a headline spans three columns and there is a rule between each column of text, the inside rules must stop at the same level.

- Subheads break up text into subsections, and carry almost as much impact as headlines. Be sure that the subheads are compatible with body text and headlines.

- Ensure every headline is set the same distance from the top of its column, and that the measurement of all body text from its headline is the same. Pay attention to whether the measurement from headline to first paragraph is the same, more, or less than that between paragraphs. Keep the application of styles consistent. This is where PageMaker's Paragraph specifications menu in conjunction with style definitions really helps.

1. With a headline selected, choose Paragraph from the Type menu.

2. Choose the amount of space below the headline by entering a value in the After box under Paragraph space. (If your measurement preferences are different than the measurement system you want to use, type your measurement as .5i for 1/2 inch, or 0p4 for 4 points.)

3. With the text selected, choose Define styles from the Type menu. It should have Selection highlighted, now click on New. This will give you an opportunity to name the selected style. You can type in Headline and replace the existing headline style.

4. Each time you select a line of text and style it as headline, the body text begins the correct distance below.

Avoid the Underline Type Style

Instead, Draw Your Own Line

HEADLINES IN ALL CAPS CAN BE HARD TO READ

Headlines Not in All Caps Can Be Easier to Read

Measure All Rules Between Columns When a Headline Spans Several

Lorem ipsum dolor sit amet, consectetuer adipiscing elit, sed diam nonummy nibh euismod tincidunt. Ut laoreet dolore magna aliquam erat volutpat. Ut wisi enim ad minim veniam, quis nostrud exerci. Tation

ullamcorper suscipit lobortis nisl ut aliquip ex ea commodo con sequat. Hendrerit in vulputate velit esse molestie consequat, vel illum dolore eu feugiat nulla facilisis at vero eros et accu Imsan et iusto odio dignissim

qui blandit praesent luptatum zzril delenit augue duis dolore te feugait nulla facilisi. Lorem ipsum dolor sit amet, consec tetuer adipiscing elit, sed diam nonummy nibh euismod tin cidunt ut laoreet dolore magna.

The use of initial caps dates back hundreds of years to when monks created illuminated manuscripts. More than simply beautiful, they help organize information and provide an additional "point of entry" that leads the reader into the text.

*K*atie is tall, slender, aristocratic looking, though she is wholly without pomp and affectation. From a photograph one might guess her to be upper-tier European royalty, but only if she isn't smiling. A laugh will shatter the illusion quickly. A true royal never would open up the way Katie does with a laugh. She is, she says, "Just a stubborn Austrian." The blood is red, not blue. And Katie is in love. Stubborn Austrian love.

*B*ernie is all scrubbed, bright-eyed, ruddy-faced Irish. From a photo, smiling or not, one would always guess him to be Irish. No chance for royalty here, though somehow it's easy to imagine a leprechaun perched on a branch of the family tree. He speaks in short bursts, Irish laconic it is called, usually in sentences no longer than the snap count for the Notre Dame quarterback. He rarely seems unhappy, save for golf games lost at the 18th hole, and the central reason is the tall, smiling Austrian he married 50 years ago. ❦

Katie's Prayer

Upon the occasion of their Golden Wedding Anniversary, Katie wrote this:

When I was about 20 years old I started praying to Saint Anthony to find me a good husband. As it happened, he chose Bun Doyle. That was his nickname at the time. They couldn't have found a better husband than Bernie. He was everything one could ask for and then more. Seeing and meeting Bernie for the first time was at a Catholic Youth Young Adults houseparty. I couldn't take my eyes off him that night and haven't since.

We became engaged at Christmas of 1940 and were married April 19, 1941, at the St. Joe Farm Parish by Father Murray.

He had just been ordained a few years before that.

I said, "Dear Lord, bless us with a beautiful daughter," which we are thankful for.

We have truly enjoyed our first 50 years together and have many, many, many lovely memories of them. The hard work, the good times, the nice travel, the vacations, the years of playing golf. May this be the year Bernie can score his age in golf and not let opponents run in long putts on number 18 to win the tournament of the day.

Besides loving God, I wonder if golf is his first or second love.

We are very proud of our lovely family, relatives, and friends. Also the wonderful clergy we have been associated with over the years. May the dear Lord bless us with continued health and happiness. We have so much to be thankful for.

Amen

The Meeting

*T*here is no question who the romantic is in the family. About the day he met Katie, Bernie remembers, "We met at a party. We were on and off for awhile." And was he, as one might suppose he would be upon seeing the person who would be his partner for half a century, immediately struck by the vision of Katie?

"Oh, yeah," chuckles Bernie. "I suppose."

And what were his thoughts that day? "That's a hard question. I don't remember back 50 years like that."

That's okay. Katie does. The year was 1939. The year of Rhett and Scarlett. And Katie and Bernie.

"We used to have what you'd call the CYO. Everyone would meet at someone else's home. We were at this big houseparty. Everyone played cards at a certain table. I was sitting in a big dining room. Bernie came in late because he always had to milk cows three times a day in those years.

"When he came in, he just really took my eye, you know. I thought, 'Boy, I wonder who

This brochure, celebrating a couple's 50th wedding anniversary, uses initial caps in the Shelley Allegro font to begin each section of text. Designer: Michael J. Nolan

There are many ways to design initial caps. Here are some thoughts about creating them:

■ Don't be timid when creating initial caps. They are extravagant by nature and should be large enough in relation to the body text to really stand out. An initial cap only two text lines high is usually not effective.

■ Give initial caps room to breathe. Don't set them too close to headlines or they will look crowded.

■ Measure initial caps carefully. Initial caps touching the letters that follow them, or those too far away, are clumsy and show inattention to detail. The same is true of caps that hover above or below the baseline of the body text. Check your spacing using 200% or 400% magnification. Be prepared to print out several laser proofs until you get it right.

■ If you are printing only black, consider using a screen value for the initial cap. Add a color of black that's less than 100% to the color palette and choose that color for the initial cap.

■ Combine fonts. Mix serif and sans serif faces. Use scripts and other specialty fonts that would not work for body text or headlines.

■ Transform letters by stretching, rotating, or other type manipulations that will draw attention to the initial cap—which is what it's supposed to do.

■ Certain rounded letters, such as the S, O or Q should sit slightly below the baseline of the body text because of the illusion created by the curve.

■ Try different methods of placement. Some initial caps can stand on the baseline of the first line of text and tower above; others can be embedded or dropped several lines down into the text. They also can be outdented or indented. (Whatever style you choose, however, ensure that you apply that style consistently throughout the publication.)

Exaggerated letters, such as this Univers Extra Black E condensed to 20% of its usual width can provide interesting variations from the ordinary. In addition, this initial cap is colored yellow, and set in a purple box which gives it even more impact, especially when contrasted against the red color of the body text.

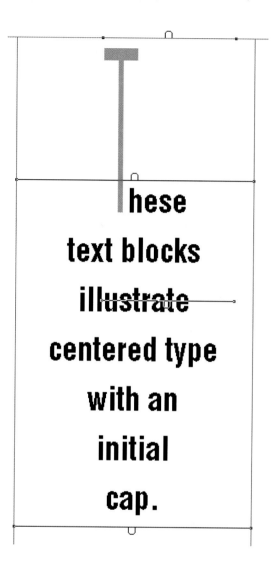

These text blocks illustrate centered type with an initial cap.

Creating initial caps

Using PageMaker, you can create initial caps as part of the body text block, or as a separate text block. They can be imported EPS files, TIFF, or PCX scans that you wrap text around, or they can be made with Aldus Addition Drop caps. No particular method is best for all situations. Let's look at some different ways you can create initial caps:

■ Standing caps as part of a text block

When you create initial caps within a text block, the key to success is proper leading. Use the steps below to create standing caps:

1. Make sure you are working in Proportional leading by opening Paragraph specifications (Control-M) and clicking on Spacing... to go to the submenu. You choose the leading method there.

2. With the Type tool, select the first character of the first word in the text block, and open Type specs... (Control-T). Change the point size to a larger specification. You also can change the font or style, but do not change the leading.

3. You may have to kern the body text in the first word closer to or farther from the initial cap. Click between the initial cap and the next letter, and press Shift-Control-left cursor arrow to close a gap, or Shift-Control-right cursor arrow to increase space.

■ Drop caps as a separate text block

Drop caps can be created either through the Aldus Addition Drop cap... or by using two text blocks. The first way is easier; but the second way offers more control. Here's how to make a drop cap three lines deep using two text blocks:

1. Flow the text block into the column, close the windowshade until only three lines appear; draw down a guideline to the bottom line of the text block. Use the lower left handle to move the left margin enough to accommodate the drop cap.

2. Pick up the rest of the text, and flow it with the top of the loaded icon aligned to the guideline you drew.

3. Cut the first letter from the first word (Control-X). With the Text tool, click and drag just outside the text block to roughly describe an area for the drop cap. Paste the letter into this new text block (Control-V); select it, and open Type specs... (Control-T) to change its specifications.

4. Change to 200% view; use the Pointer tool on the left-hand bottom handle of the first three lines of text to adjust it closer to or away from the drop cap.

5. Use the Pointer tool to adjust the guideline to the baseline of the third line of type. Click on the drop cap and adjust it vertically until it shares the same baseline.

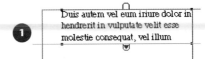

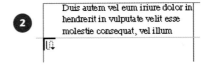

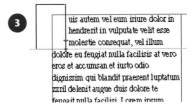

Imported letters, scans, or drawings

You can also create initial caps in programs such as Aldus FreeHand or Adobe Illustrator, or they can be scanned images saved in TIFF or EPS formats. Use these methods when you want an elaborate, multicolored letter that incorporates graphics. They are also good for creating initial caps that lie underneath the text rather than beside it.

orem ipsum dolor sit amet,

tincidunt ut laoreet dolore r

nostrud exerci tation ullamc

Duis autem vel eum iriure c

dolore eu feugiat nulla facil

praesent luptatum zzril dele

amet, consectetuer adipisc

magna aliquam erat volutpa

The initial cap in this example was created in Aldus Freehand with a 20% fill. Then it was imported into PageMaker, and placed behind the text.

Automated drop caps

The Aldus Additions Drop cap... provides a simple solution if you are using drop caps repeatedly throughout a publication. It is routine and does not involve as much careful measurement as other methods. Here's how it works:

1. Using the Text tool, select the letter for the drop cap.

2. Pull down the Utilities Menu to Aldus Additions and choose Drop cap.

3. Enter a value in the Size category for the number of lines deep you want the cap placed. Click on OK and the program will automatically change the letter to a point size appropriate for that number of lines.

The Drop cap feature of Aldus Additions uses a combination of line breaks, superscript position and type size to create a drop cap. The easiest way to remove a drop cap is to insert the text cursor in the paragraph, select the addition and click remove.

Tables, coupons, pricelists, numbered lists, and bulleted lists utilize indents and tabs. You should know the difference between decimal, centered, left- and right-aligned tabs, and know how to use tab leaders. When you can work confidently with the Indents/tabs menu, you are well on your way to becoming a PageMaker expert.

The Indents/tabs ruler

To affect the tab settings for any paragraph, you must first select the text and use the Text tool. Because indents and tabs work on a full paragraph, it is not necessary that you select all the words, only that you locate the cursor in the paragraph somewhere. Once you identify the paragraph with the cursor, open the Indents/tabs ruler by typing Control-I, or by selecting Indents/tabs from the Type menu.

Copying tab specs

To apply the correct tab specs from one paragraph to the following paragraph, use the Text tool to select a line with the proper tab settings; drag down through the text to select the text to which you want to apply the preceding specs. Type Control-I, or select Indents/tabs from the Type menu. As soon as the ruler opens, click OK. The correct tabs will be applied to the new text.

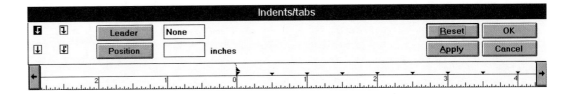

When you click the reset button on the Indents/tabs ruler, tabs return to the default setting of one every half inch.

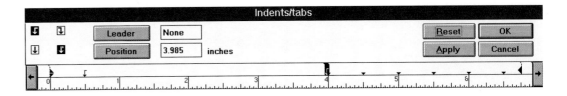

To change tab type, select the tab on the ruler and click one of the four choices: left-aligned, right-aligned, centered, or decimal. Here a left-aligned tab is being changed to a decimal tab.

Creating hanging indents

You can see hang bullets throughout this book where small squares precede text indented along its left margin. Working with the tab ruler to perform this function can be tricky. The key is to press the Shift key when trying to get the bottom half of the double arrow to move independently of the top half. To make hanging indents, use the following steps:

1. Use the Text tool to select the paragraph you want to apply the hanging indents.

2. Holding the Shift key down, click the Pointer tool on the bottom portion of the double arrow.

3. Drag the bottom half of the arrow across the ruler and stop at the point you wish to indent the first line after the bullet, and all succeeding lines.

4. After you have the bottom half of the double arrow in place, position a left-hand tab on top of it. This is where the first line of your text will begin. To type a hanging indent, type (bullet)-tab-(first letter of text).

5. Click on the OK button.

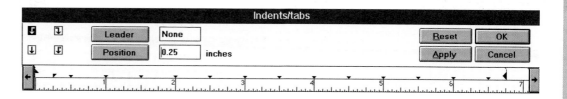

To create a hanging indent, first use the Shift key to "unlock" the bottom part of the double arrows, drag it in towards the right, where it will represent the left position for the second and all succeeding lines of text in a paragraph.

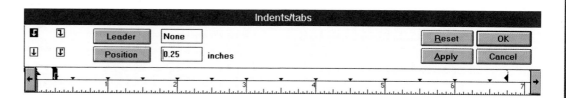

The second step is to place a left-tab in the same position as where the succeeding lines of text will align. When entering your text, you type the bullet first, then a tab so the first letter of the first line will align with the succeeding lines.

TYPE

Creating coupons

You can find coupons in all types of documents—from flyers to brochures. If created skillfully, they can add to the professional appearance of the publication. Use the following guidelines when designing them:

■ If you include a coupon in a document, it should be easy to fill out. Don't waste space with large type for the name, address, or city labels. These can be set in a small point size and remain perfectly readable—because readers have an expectation of what the labels will say.

■ If you want respondents to include their area code with phone numbers, indicate that in "shorthand" by placing parentheses as part of the line.

■ You can use dotted lines to separate the coupon from the rest of the copy on the page, or you can use a less traditional means for setting them off, as you see here.

■ It is helpful to have a lead-in line to a coupon, something like, "Yes! I would love to receive a free copy of...." In such a case, make the Yes large and stylish.

■ Pay attention to where you place a coupon. If the reader cuts it out, the page behind it is destroyed. If the reader is to keep the document, make sure what's lost behind the coupon is not something important.

■ Many desktop-published documents use the Zapf Dingbat letter q when a checkbox is needed. While this drop-shadowed box can be an appropriate choice, in most instances a checkbox without the drop shadow is a simpler and more elegant solution. You can create the checkbox by typing the solid Zapf Dingbat letter n, selecting it, and choosing the Outline style.

On the left is the Zapf Dingbat letter n with the outline style. On the right is the more commonly-used Zapf Dingbat letter q—a desktop publishing cliché.

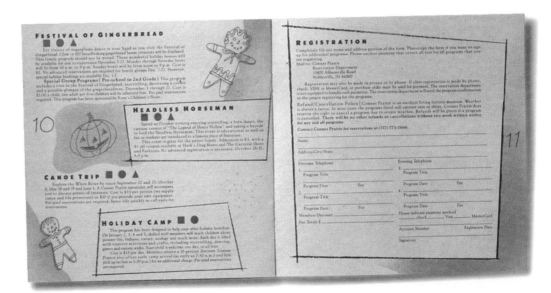

The example above shows an effective coupon that does not rely on the traditional dotted line. Designers: Laura Lacy-Sholly & James Sholly Antenna, Indianapolis Client: Conner Prairie

Creating coupons with tabs

You can create a quick and versatile coupon using tab settings and leaders to create the lines. The best aspect of this technique is that the coupon is a unified text block, and doesn't require the tiresome measuring when using the Line tool. Here is how it works:

1. Type the information you want filled out in the coupon, and type a tab after each category (such as Name, Address, etcetera). Enter a return following the tab each time you want a new line.

2. Select all the text where lines are needed.

3. Choose Indents/tabs under the Type menu.

4. Place a right tab at the end of the line by clicking the right tab icon and clicking the cursor in the desired position on the tab ruler.

5. Select the leader style desired—in this case, a solid line.

6. For lines with more than one category (such as City, State, Zip in this example), select the line separately (triple-clicking selects an entire line) and place a tab stop in each location desired.

7. Experiment with the tab locations to get the right amount of distance between categories.

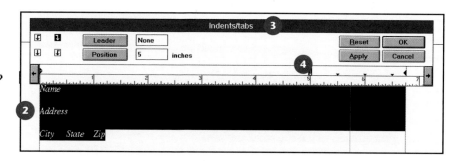

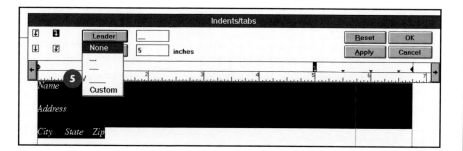

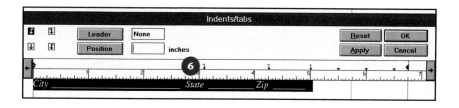

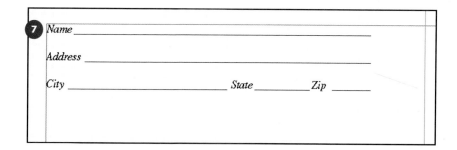

Numbered lists

There are some special considerations for the treatment of numbered lists:

■ If you have a numbered list with more than nine entries, make sure that the position for the numbers is set with decimal tabs rather than flush left. This is because the first digit in two-digit numbers needs to move out to the left.

■ It is very effective to treat the numbers like drop caps—especially if there are not many items in the numbered list. (If the publication is informal enough to do so.) Second color adds a nice touch. (See top right example.)

■ Numbers also can be used like headlines, centered above lines of text below the numbers. (See bottom right example.)

■ There is no limit to how many points can be in a numbered list. If you have more than 12, don't use a design element that will become too repetitive and tiring.

1 Lorem ipsum dolor sit a consectetuer adipiscing nonummy nibh euismod tin laoreet dolore magna aliqua volutpat ut wisi enim ad mi

2 Quis nostrud exerci tat ullamcorper suscipit lo aliquip ex ea commodo cons

3 Duis autem vel eum iri hendrerit in vulputate molestie consequat, vel illu feugiat.

1

Lorem ipsum dolor sit amet, consectetuer adipiscing elit, sed diam nonummy nibh euismod tincidunt.

2

Ut laoreet dolore magna aliquam erat volutpat.

3

Ut wisi enim ad minim veniam, quis nostrud exerci.

4

Tation ullamcorper suscipit lobortis nisl ut aliquip ex ea commodo consequat.

Bulleted lists

Bullet points are effective when handled correctly—and tiresome if treated in a clumsy or sloppy fashion. Although they seem simple, there are important considerations to remember when using them:

- Balance the bullet size to the text. You want neither undersized or overpowering bullets. Control-Shift-8 in most fonts gives you a nice, round bullet.

- Zapf Dingbats make interesting bullets. Consider squares (as you see here), triangles, or other geometric forms. Checkmarks, arrows, and similar bullets, although sometimes interesting, can become boring if overused.

- If you have too many bullet points, the reader becomes distracted. With more than ten points, it's better to treat the bullets as a numbered list, if appropriate, or integrate the points into the body of text.

- Never use only one or two bullet points. Bullets can look misplaced unless there are at least three separate ideas.

- Hanging bullets are very effective in setting off points. The second and all succeeding lines of text fall under the indent of the first line; the bullet "hangs" out beyond the text. (Like it does here.)

- If you are using two colors, consider printing the bullet in the second color.

Aldus Addition Bullets and numbering...

This Aldus Addition is very useful for inserting bullets and numbers in front of individual paragraphs comprising a list. It is very simple to apply. Here's how it works for adding bullets:

1. With the Text tool, select all the paragraphs that you will include in the list.

2. From the Utilities menu, open the Aldus Additions Bullets and numbering....

3. You will see five different types of bullets from which to choose. If you wish to alter these by changing point size, font, or character, you can do so after clicking on the Edit... box.

4. Click OK. The correct bullet and a tab will be inserted at the start of each paragraph.

5. To adjust the tabs, select the paragraphs and open Indents/tabs... and make the desired changes.

6. If you wish to remove the bullets, select the paragraphs, open the Addition again, and click on Remove.

To create a numbered list, follow the steps outlined above, and choose Numbers after you open the Addition. You will not be able to choose the font or point size of the numbers, but you can add a separator following the numbers such as 1., 1), 1] or 1:.

Pull-quotes, like headlines and initial caps, provide another point of entry for the reader. Think of how many times you have skimmed through a magazine or other publication, and read a pull quote that literally pulled you into reading the entire article.

You can use pull quotes to break up an otherwise monotonous text-heavy page, or they can be used to entice the reader. Regardless of the reason, the designer must be careful when creating them not to usurp the role of the editor. What you choose to emphasize on a page can change the intent of the author. This is not a decision to be taken lightly.

There are many ways to design pull quotes. Here's one of them:

1. Select the text from body copy that you want to use as a pull quote and copy it to the clipboard (Control-C).

2. Off the edge of the page, draw the approximate size of the pull quote's text block (dragging with the mouse button held down.)

3. Release the mouse button and paste the copied text into the newly-described text block (Control-V).

This annual report makes extensive use of pull quotes as points of entry to draw the reader in.
Designer: Deborah Reinerio, Red Hot Designs, San Francisco
Client: O'Connor Hospital Foundation

4. Select all the text (Control-A).

5. Choose Type specs from the Type menu and select the new font, point size, alignment, color, and other specifications for the pull quote.

6. Using the Pointer tool, click on the text block for the pull quote and drag it over the body text. Measure, align, and adjust the text block until it is in the right position.

7. Create a paper-filled, no lines rectangle that extends beyond the handles of the pull quote's text block. Send the rectangle to the back (Control-B).

8. While you still have the rectangle selected, choose Text wrap... from the Element menu, and specify . This will result in the body text flowing around the rectangle, while the pull quote text should fit inside. (If the pull quote is also wrapped outside, you may have to adjust the handles of the rectangle until the pull quote completely fits inside the rectangle, without being repelled.)

Typographer's quotation marks

Proper typographer's quotation marks and apostrophes are one of the small details which can make a project look professional. You can get them several different ways:

1. Choose Preferences from the Edit menu, and click on Other to go to the submenu.

2. Choose Use typographer's quotes and click on the OK button.

3. If you really need to type inch marks (or the single prime character) go the same dialog box and turn the feature off temporarily.

Or:

1. For opening quotes, type Shift-Conrol-[; for closing quotes, type Shift-Option-].

2. For opening single quote, type Control-[; for closing single quote or apostrophe, type Control-].

The final way is to check the Convert quotes box when you place text that was written in a word-processing program.

Never use "inch marks" to put text in "quotes!"

Rules and underlines

Sometimes lines, or rules, are necessary to add structure and order to a page. When you use rules with finesse, they can add grace and elegance to a publication.

When using rules as part of a page design, consider the following:

- Restrict your palette of rules to one or two different styles.

- Consider printing the rules in a second color. If you're printing in black only, you could make the rules using a gray screen.

- If you are using a rule structure on one page of a publication, you should keep it consistent throughout the document. Set rules on the master pages. Cover them with paper-colored boxes when they need to be removed from individual pages.

- Rules used to lead from captions to a graphic should be handled so they are not confused with column rules. Use a different weight or color for them.

- Think of rules that are not strictly rules: rectangles, dotted lines (of any size), or lines made of leader.

Rules made of tab leader

Rules can be created by using tab leader. (You may want to refer to Indents/tabs for further understanding on page 99.) You can create Tab leader rules using the following steps:

1. Measure the height for the dotted-line rules.

2. With the Text tool, create a new text block the same width as the height you've just measured. Create the approximate width with the mouse button held down as you drag. When you release the button, you will have a flashing cursor in an "invisible" text block.

3. Type x-Tab-x-Return and open Indents/tabs in the Type menu.

4. Place a right-hand tab at the end of the line, and while you have it selected, pull down the leader heading and choose Custom. Enter a letter, number, or other character to use as the leader. Change the font, style, and size of this character by selecting the text block with the Type tool and choosing Type specs.

5. Remove the x from the beginning and end of the line.

6. Using the Pointer tool, select the text block and choose text rotation. Place the rotated text block in the correct location inside a column guide.

7. Copy the text block, power paste (Control-Shift-P) the copy on top of the original; hold the Shift key and move the copy to the next location.

Setting the weight of rules

You can now specify Rule widths from .1 to hundreds of points.

1. With a line selected, pull down the Element menu, and choose Custom under Line.

2. Choose the style of line you want to use.

3. Type in a value for Line weight.

4. Click on the OK button.

Automatic rules

You can set Rules to automatically print a specified distance above or below type in the Paragraph menu. (See "Creating reverses as a style", page 80 for further explanation of paragraph rules.)

Horizontal rules

Thin rules often are used between columns of text to delineate them. Another use—more interesting because it is seen less—is to use thick horizontal rules above or below stories. Utilize color if you have that option. If your job is one color, they can be screened gray. If full-strength black, they may be too distracting. Also, if you are using horizontal rules, you probably should not use vertical rules. You can get too much of a good thing.

Reverse rules

The capability to make reverse rules means that you can place the rules on a solid color background. If you use this technique, don't make the reverse rule too thin or it will fill in during printing. A width of one point is safe—anything less is risky.

Intersecting rules

Care must be taken to measure rules perfectly where they intersect; it looks bad to have rules that meet improperly. Here again, 200% or 400% page view will allow for precise measurement.

Using rules with type

It is rarely acceptable to use the underline feature found under Type specs, because the lines are drawn beneath the type without regard to descenders, commas, or spaces—with no control over color, placement, line weight, or other stylistic considerations. Underlining is simply an old typewriter convention that was used to indicate italics before it was possible to type italics. Now that we have the capability to do real type-setting, you should use italics wherever body copy is underlined. If someone has supplied text that contains underlining, the steps below describe how to use Story editor to change all the underlines to italics:

1. Click on the text block with either the Pointer tool or the Text tool; open Story editor under the Edit menu.

2. Choose Change (also under the Edit menu), and click on Attributes. (You may want to choose All stories before clicking on Attributes if you need to search more than one text block.)

3. Under Find, pull down the Type style menu and choose Underline.

4. Under Change, pull down the Type style menu and choose Italic.

5. Click on the OK button, and either select Change all or Find followed by Change & find. The latter is a more time-consuming method, but will ensure that you don't inadvertently change something that should not be changed.

Styles

Another brilliant feature of PageMaker is the styles palette. With it, you can achieve great speed and accuracy when creating layouts. If you need to make a global change to a recurring element, it can be done with a few keystrokes.

Style definition

A style is a set of specifications that you can apply to a paragraph—a block of text that ends when you press a return—that formats the text for font, point size, leading, indents, tabs, and paragraph specifications.

Creating styles

Styles are easily created. You begin with the simple Define styles... command found under the Type menu (or Control-3). When the dialog box opens, you can select any category, such as Body text, and choose Edit. You'll see a submenu that enables you to change the specifications for Type, Paragraph, Tabs, or Hyphenation. You'll recognize the dialog boxes for each of these, because they are the same as those found under the menus of the same name.

You can get to the second dialog box quickly by double-clicking on the category you wish to edit.

It is also possible to create a new style based on an existing paragraph. Here's how it's done:

1. Place text cursor in the paragraph that will be the basis for your new style.

2. Open the Define styles... dialog box (Control-3).

3. The selection will be highlighted. Click on New. If you want the new specifications to replace an existing style, type the name of that style exactly as it currently appears in the style palette.

4. Click on the OK button. The specifications of your paragraph will overwrite the previous specifications for that style.

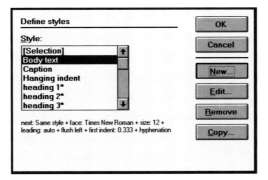

Copying styles

When you want to copy a style sheet from another publication, click on Copy... in the Define styles dialog box and locate the publication that you want to copy from. This will globally copy the entire style sheet from the publication; it is not possible to copy individual styles.

Importing styles

When importing word processed text from a program that does not support style sheets, you can identify individual styles by typing a style-name tag in front of each paragraph where a style change is to take place. You must have predefined these styles in your PageMaker file before importing the text. (To find out more about this, see page 87.)

Applying styles

Once you have defined styles, it is simple to apply them to any paragraph or group of paragraphs. In either Edit or Layout view, place the text cursor in a paragraph, or select a group of paragraphs, and click on the desired style in the Style palette. If the style palette is not displayed, choose it from the Windows menu.

Another quick way to assign styles is to place the cursor in your text, and pull down the Type menu to Style, drag through the submenu and release on the style you want to assign.

If you have a long word-processed document that will contain many different styles after placement in PageMaker, you may want to begin by applying one style, (Body text) to the entire document. Next, go back and reassign the appropriate headline, subhead, caption, and other styles on a line-by-line basis to the document.

You may find it frustrating that you cannot assign more than one style to an individual paragraph, (for instance a Zapf Dingbat bullet point followed by a Stone Sans subhead). In this case, set the style for the text, set a placeholder letter for the bullet, and go through later and paste a copied dingbat over that letter.

If, after applying a style, you make a change to the formatted text, such as bolding a word or adding a dingbat in a line, a plus sign will appear on that style name in the style palette when you select that text.

If you apply a style to a paragraph that you've already formatted with bold, italic, etcetera, hold the Shift key when assigning the style and the locally placed formatting will not be dropped.

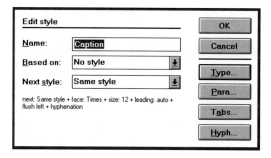

Editing styles

You've laid out the entire publication and discovered that there's too much text to fit in using 12 point type. It's very simple to open the Define styles... menu and edit Body text to a smaller point size, or to reduce the leading, change the tracking, etc. Simply select the style name you want to change, click on Edit... and change its specifications. It will take a moment or two for all the text in your document to recompose.

A very quick method for editing styles is to hold down the Control key and click on the style name in the style palette you want to edit. You will immediately see the editing dialog box.

Next styles

When inputting text in PageMaker, it is useful to have the style for the next line change automatically after you type a return. For example, when you type a Subhead, the next line of copy after the return should be Body text. You can accomplish this by opening the Edit... submenu after opening Define styles..., and designating the next style to follow.

With the introduction of the Story Editor in PageMaker version 4.0, the program became a serious tool for creating documentation. Features such as spell checking, search and replace, and other text handling capabilities make mastery of the Story Editor a must for the expert user of PageMaker.

Accessing Story Editor

You can access the Story Editor by choosing it when you pull down the Edit menu, or by typing Control-E. Typing Control-E works as a toggle switch, taking you back and forth between word-processing clarity and the Layout view of your page. When working with small type (like 6-point Helvetica Condensed), this can be very useful.

The menu bar of PageMaker is different when you are in Story Editor. Take time to explore all the options while in Story Editor; although some of them have the same names as their equivalent Layout view menus, they perform different functions. You can perform the following functions while in Story Editor:

■ Find

If you don't know where a particular word or paragraph is in your document, you can choose the word, or an attribute you know is in the paragraph and go to that place by checking the All stories option in the Find dialog box. Once you have found a word in a story, highlight it, and press Control-E (or Edit layout from the Edit menu). PageMaker will turn to the correct page in Layout view and highlight the word.

■ Find by attribute

The capability to search by attribute is extremely useful. You can use it to restrict PageMaker's search actions to text with a specific format or combination of formats. Here is how it works:

1. In Story Edit view, select Find from the Utilities menu.

2. Click on Attributes… to go to the next dialog box where you can specify which attributes (such as a particular font, bold or italic words, etcetera) to find.

3. Choose any attribute or combination of attributes for the search.

4. Click on the OK button.

Change

Change is a more powerful find. Here are some changes you should perform on text routinely:

- Search for double spaces and replace them with single spaces. Many diehard typists insist that two spaces are needed to separate sentences in text, and in typing class, that was true. Typesetters always place one space between a period and the sentence following it. To do otherwise leads to what are known as "rivers" of text. (This condition is aggravated when text is justified.) You may need to search two or three times, depending on the quality of the original word-processed text. Some keyboarders will place three or four spaces to create indents, or when creating charts place extra spaces to put text into columns. Replacing double spaces with single spaces may still leave double spaces after a first check.

- Search for space-period, and replace with period space; also search for space-comma, and replace with comma space.

- You also may need to search for space-dash-space, or dash-dash, and replace with em- or en-dashes (Control-Shift-= or Control-=.)

- You can use Attributes to change fonts. For instance, to change all occurrences of Times Roman to Helvetica.

Spelling

Spell checking is not a substitute for proofreading, but rather augments it. Clearly, a spell checker would not alert you to "now" as a misspelled word. How would it know that you really meant "know"? Spell checking also functions well as a double check against words typed without a space between them, or to check the spelling of unfamiliar words on the spot. Here is how you can perform a spellcheck:

1. In Story Edit view, choose Spelling from the Edit menu, or type Control-L.

2. The dialog box will ask if you want to check the selected text, current story, all stories, or all open publications. If there is just one word you are unsure of, select it by double-clicking on it and choose selected text for a spell check.

3. Whenever a misspelled word is found, PageMaker will suggest alternatives. If you see the correct word, double click on it and it will replace the one in question.

Changing Story Edit view font

If you are working on a small screen or there is a glare on your monitor, you may benefit from changing the font and/or point size of text in Story view under the Preferences menu.

Displaying paragraphs and tabs

In checking the small details that give documents that professional look, it is important that all columns and indents are set with tabs rather than spaces. To check this, you can ask for a display of returns and tabs either under the Other section of the Preferences menu, or by pulling down the Options menu while you are in Story Edit view and choosing Display ¶. Returns will be indicated with ¶, and arrows will show tabs. You can quickly scan your story in Story Edit view to determine if you have placed tab stops and returns appropriately.

Using arrow keys

The arrow keys on the Macintosh can be used to move your cursor rapidly through text in Story Edit and Layout views. Once you are accustomed to using them, you can fly through text editing tasks with lightning speed. Here are a few tricks when using the arrow keys to move the cursor:

- Holding the Alt key while pressing the right or left arrow key, moves you through a document a word at a time.

- Holding the Shift key while pressing the right or left arrow key, selects letters as you move through them.

- Holding the Shift and Alt keys together, while pressing the right or left arrow key, selects one word one at a time.

TYPE

One feature has remained constant through each version of PageMaker and that is the concept of text blocks and windowshades. Once understood, the windowshades work very well—but they can be tricky. Version 5.0 contains some powerful new features that address some of the shortcomings of the old windowshade.

Working with text blocks

Think of text blocks like graphics. Focus on the shape of text blocks rather than what they contain. Move and resize text blocks using the Pointer tool.

There are two basic ways to alter text blocks: with the Text tool and with the Pointer tool. With the Text tool, you can edit text, change the font, point size, width, or other characteristics of the type inside a text block. With the Pointer tool, you can flow text into columns, change the width of columns, or force text into another column, or onto another page.

Consider these tips when manipulating text blocks:

■ If you accidentally click on a text block windowshade with the Pointer tool and pick up an unintended "loaded" text icon, simply click on another tool in the Toolbox and the loaded icon disappears.

■ If you have measured the vertical alignment of a text block already, but want to change its column width, use the bottom handles. This keeps the vertical placement unchanged.

■ It is sometimes necessary to combine two text blocks into one. This is easy to do. Click into the text block with the Text tool, and Select All (Control-A). Cut what you have selected (Control-X). Click an insertion point into the other text block, and paste (Control-V). The text you cut now flows into the remaining text block.

Find overset text

Overset text refers to text windowshades that have not been pulled down completely. There is an Aldus Addition for finding overset text, and it reminds me of fax machines: we didn't know we needed them until we had them. This Addition is a surefire way to ensure that you will never again suffer the embarrassment of a column whose last two lines have disappeared because a new line was typed before it. Here is how Find overset text works:

1. After you finish laying out all text for the publication, choose Find overset text from the Aldus Additions menu under Utilities. (It does not matter what tool you are using.)

2. If there is a text block windowshade that you have not completely pulled down, Addition takes you to that page and displays the text handle in red.

3. Pull down the handle to completely reveal the remaining text.

4. The Addition does not automatically move on to the next occurrence of overset text. You must repeat the process until you get the message that there is no more overset text found.

Add cont'd line...

This feature is one of the Aldus Additions found under the Utilities menu. It can save time at the end of a project when you are rushing to add all the final touches, such as the "continued to" and "continued from" information. It creates a consistent method for directing the reader when stories jump from one page to another. One caution is that if a story's location changes after you have run this Addition, the information will not automatically update; you must rerun the process. You can even customize the continuation type style and format. Here is how the Continuation Addition works:

1. Go to the beginning page for a story that continues to another page, and select its last column with the Pointer tool.

2. Under the Utilities menu, choose Aldus Additions and Add cont'd line....

3. Choose Bottom of textblock to insert a continuation notice reading "Continued on page (n)" and click on the OK button.

4. Addition automatically inserts the correct continuation information in a new text block just below the one you selected and puts a continuation style into the style palette. (You may change the style by using the Define Styles command.)

5. You may need to readjust windowshades to display text correctly. Use this opportunity to draw a horizontal guideline where the text block ends. Use that guideline to align the continuation block.

6. Move to the page where the story continues and repeat the process, checking Top of textblock to get the "Continued from page (n)" line.

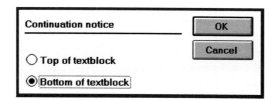

Traversing text blocks

A story continued over several pages can be difficult to work on in Layout view. Another Aldus Addition enables you to move from where it leaves off on one page to where it begins on the next, to work backwards through it, or to find its beginning or end. Traversing text blocks works flawlessly as described below:

1. In layout view, click on a text block.

2. Choose Traverse text blocks from the Aldus Additions submenu under the Utilities menu.

3. Choose the text you want to view in the dialog box and click on the OK button. Layout view automatically moves to the page with the text block you have chosen.

TYPE

111

Hyphenation is one of those important details that make for a quality document. Understanding the subtleties of hyphenation is very important; fortunately, PageMaker can help if you know where to look.

After you lay out the text in columns and edit for the final time, scan the columns for bad hyphenation. Words that break in funny places, large gaps, too many hyphens in a row—all these are hyphenations that you should change. Here are a few guidelines:

■ Avoid leaving a widow or orphan—a single word or part of a word—on a line by itself. To make a premature or abrupt ending to the line above the widow, insert the cursor in front of the word and type Shift-Return to move another word down to the last line. This is a soft return that moves the entire word to the next line without activating other paragraph attributes such as indents and line spacing.

Another solution may be selecting words in the last two lines of your paragraph and tightening the tracking to get the last syllable(s) into the preceding line.

■ Three consecutive lines with hyphens is too many, and if more than a third of all lines in a paragraph are hyphenated, that's too many as well. Solutions may include the discretionary hyphen (Control-hyphen) just before the first character of a word you do not want hyphenated); increasing or decreasing the tracking on words or groups of words; changing the hyphenation zone; or changing the hyphenation in a paragraph from automatic to manual and hyphenating words individually when it appears appropriate to do so. Manual hyphenation can be selected by following these steps:

1. Select the paragraph or paragraphs where you want to change hyphenation.

2. Open the Hyphenation submenu under the Type menu.

3. To change the hyphenation zone, type in a new value. If you choose a larger value, more words will hyphenate—a smaller value allows fewer words to hyphenate.

4. To hyphenate any word, choose Manual and click on the OK button. In layout view, scan the right side of your columns at 200% view and wherever you want a word to hyphenate (from a line to the line above it), place your cursor in the word that you want to hyphenate and hold down the Control key and the hyphen key.

In the Hyphenation dialog box, you can choose to turn hyphenation on or off, make it a manual option, limit the number of consecutive hyphens, or change the hyphenation zone.

Cleaning up the rag

Rag refers to the unevenness of lines when text is left or right aligned. Some unevenness is desirable, but too much can be distracting. In this area attention to detail pays off with a subtle, but important impact on the overall appearance of your publication.

Clean up the rag by scanning the right side of each column and placing soft returns (hold down the Shift and Return keys) in front of small words that extend out too far. You also can use discretionary hyphens where you want words to move to the next line. Clean up the rag at 200% view, moving down the page by holding down the Alt key and the mouse button while dragging through the columns. The examples below illustrate how repositioning a couple of small words at the end of line 3 and line 8 (in the left paragraph) achieve a smoother look (see the right paragraph).

consecutive lines of text end
: at the end of three lines in a
ny, and if more than a third of
are hyphenated, that's too
: solutions if you have many
column? They might involve
; the tracking on words or
ng the hyphenation zone, or
nation in a paragraph to
1g words individually when it
at is done as follows:

· consecutive lines of text end
s at the end of three lines in a
any, and if more than a third
oh are hyphenated, that's too
e solutions if you have many
column? They might involve
; the tracking on words or
ing the hyphenation zone,
henation in a paragraph to
1g words individually when
That is done as follows:

The photograph on this calendar looks at familiar objects in a new way—a great technique for creating effective graphics.
Designer: Jennifer Morla, San Francisco
Client: American President Companies

Graphics are essential for making a page design memorable. They can be used purely for decorative purposes, or they can convey information to the reader. The best graphics accomplish both things.

The capability to juxtapose graphics and text set PageMaker apart from the word processing software that preceded it—and created a new discipline, desktop publishing. PageMaker's graphics handling for Windows has come a long way since 1987.

Finding quality graphics for your publication is one of the primary challenges you face when using PageMaker. Rarely does even the best designer create all the graphics used in a document. Illustrations, photographs, charts, diagrams, and other graphics often come from many different sources.

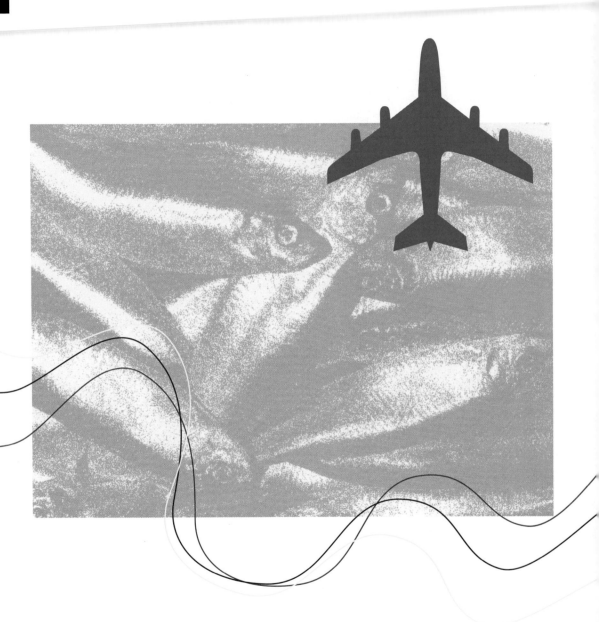

Combining graphics with text is one of the primary functions of PageMaker. However, the program is not designed for creating graphics other than simple boxes, backgrounds, rules, or the like. The best graphics are scanned, drawn in other programs such as Aldus FreeHand or Adobe Illustrator, and then placed, resized, rotated, lightened, or otherwise adjusted as needed in Page-Maker. Sometimes taking the conventional approach and having graphics physically pasted into artwork or stripped into film by your printer rather than as electronic files is the best choice. This is especially true for photographs.

Incorporating graphics into a design should not be an afterthought. If you find yourself searching for last-minute clip art to make a page prettier, you're probably on the wrong track. It's much better to lay out a page with the graphics in mind when you begin.

There are numerous sources for graphic enhancements to your pages, depending on your budget, talent, time frame, and imagination. Let's look at some of them.

Photography

Photography is a common source for graphics. Photographs lend immediacy to a topic, and tell a story with a level of accuracy that illustrations seldom match.

■ **Stock photos**

Numerous companies publish catalogs containing photographs which can be purchased. They offer thousands of images, arranged by category, and just looking through the catalogs can ignite your imagination. Some stock catalog companies are now offering photos on CD-ROM, that can be searched by keywords, subjects, artist, and so forth. You can use scanned photos from a catalog to create comps for selling your client on a particular image, or use low-resolution versions off a CD. The stock company will send you the original or high-resolution file by overnight delivery if you decide to purchase the photo rights.

It is never permissible to use scans of stock photographs for final reproduction on any kind of publication, regardless of how much a scan has been altered or distorted. This is a violation of the copyright law.

Some stock photo companies that offer catalogs are:

Allstock
(206) 282-8116

Peter Arnold, Inc.
(800) 289-7468

Bettman
(212) 777-6200

Comstock
(800) 225-2727

Leo de Wys, Inc.
(800) 284-3399

FPG International
(212) 777-4210

Ibid, Inc.
(312) 733-8000

The Image Bank
(212) 529-6700

Photovault
(415) 552-9682

The Stock Market
(800) 999-0800

Third Coast Stock
(800) 323-9337

Vintage Images
(703) 207-9888

Westlight
(800) 872-7872

Sources

Commissioned photos

Many photographers specialize. Some only work in studios, others do portraits on location. Some photograph food exclusively, others architecture. Styles vary markedly, and you should always see a portfolio of a photographer's work before you contract to work with one.

It can be rewarding to work with a professional photographer—and hard work too—to get exactly the right photographs for your publication. You must be well prepared and use the photographer's time well. Have a clear idea what you want in terms of color, lighting conditions, subjects, and other variables before you arrange the photography shoot. To have to do a reshoot is expensive—and causes delays.

Photo CD

Kodak Photo CD technology has made it even easier to incorporate photos into a publication. You can take any group of slides, (or soon, 4" x 5" transparencies), and have them placed on a Photo CD when the film is developed, or if you cannot yet locate such a service, send them out to a service bureau for scanning and placement onto a Photo CD.

You can import Photo CD images into PageMaker. Low-resolution images can be placed in your document for a quicker working file and faster proof printing. Later, when the file is sent for final output, the images can be replaced with their high-resolution counterparts. To import images directly from Photo CD, follow these steps:

1. Choose Place from the File menu.

2. Locate the Photo CD, select Overview, PCD file, and click on the OK button.

3. In the Photo CD filter v.1.0 dialog box, specify color format and resolution desired.

4. Click OK to place the file.

5. Click on the page where you want to place the image.

Non-professional photos

Often, a designer is called upon to work with existing photographs. This can be a challenge because the photos supplied by a client may be of varied quality. Photos of different people featured in the same article may be different sizes, have different backgrounds, lighting conditions, and so forth. The best design solution in this case may be to scatter the photos throughout the article so they don't invite comparison. They should all be the same size (unless one person is more important to the story than the others), and should be cropped appropriately to eliminate distracting backgrounds.

Photo retouching

Before the advent of electronic publishing technology, photo retouching was an expensive process only performed by professionals. Now, with Adobe Photoshop, Aldus PhotoStyler, or Micrografx Picture Publisher, you can change backgrounds, montage images, do color correction, blur, sharpen, take out troublesome details, and perform many other manipulations. This can result in humorous juxtapositions, dramatic combinations, or simply improvement of a questionable photo.

Commissioned art

Like photographers, every city has illustrators who specialize in different subjects, techniques, and media. In developing illustrations for your publication, some may require a lot of direction to produce what you want, while others will be able to grasp your idea immediately and come up with a terrific solution. In either case, you should see rough sketches first, before an illustration is completely developed. When assigning illustrations, it is important to specify the intended proportions, size, and placement of the illustration on the page.

Clip art

Clip art refers to ready-made illustrations, either as hard copy or on disk, that you can add to publications. There is a tremendous amount of useful clip art available. Quality varies widely, and many images are seen repeatedly in print. One reliable source is any of the excellent Dover books or disks of copyright-free art. Dover can be reached at (516) 294-7000.

Mills-Peninsula Hospital Foundation
1991 Annual Report

Both the woman and the wall she is sitting on are copyright-free clip art from Dover.

The dramatic "Thank You" script on the left was commissioned art provided by a calligrapher, scanned, and traced in Adobe Illustrator, and imported into PageMaker as an EPS file. It was then foil stamped when the piece was printed. Designer/Calligrapher: Deborah Reinerio Red Hot Designs, San Francisco Client: Mills-Peninsula Hospital Foundation

Video images

If your Macintosh is properly configured with a video capture card and associated software, you can take still frame "grabs" from VCRs, camcorders, broadcast or cable television, or from a still video camera for use as graphics. (If you use grabs from commercial sources for publication, you may be infringing on copyright laws.) Most video sources are analog—data as a continually fluctuating voltage rather than discrete pieces of information—and the frame grabber converts them into a digital format like other Macintosh graphics.

Most frame grabbers either save images as TIFF or have a plug-in module for direct input into programs such as Aldus PhotoStyler or Adobe Photoshop. If this plug-in is a TWAIN module you can use it with any TWAIN compliant image editing program. You can save the images from these programs as TIFF for later placement into PageMaker.

Portrait of Jackson
© 1988 Michael Nolan
This image was originally a video scan capturing a live subject through the MacVision video interface. Here, a laser print was scanned and saved as a TIFF file. The large scan was lightened in Image control… and the small magenta image was changed to black and white, which is why it appears transparent. Each scan was assigned a color in the color palette.

Screen captures

When you are in any program on the PC, you can take a snapshot of whatever the screen is displaying. This screen capture can be imported into PageMaker for use as a graphic, whether in black and white or color. (Many of the figures in this book are screen captures.)

If you have a color monitor and do not have graphics software, you can change the desktop pattern on your screen display and make a capture of the pattern and place it into PageMaker (like the figures on this page). To change the desktop display pattern, open the Control Panel and double click on Desktop. Choose the Wallpaper setting and then select one of the available patterns. (Note that any .bmp files located in your Windows directory will show up here. These .bmp files can be created and edited in the Paintbrush application that ships with Windows as well as most image-editing and paint programs.)

The resolution of screen captures is that of your screen which will usually range from 700 to 100 dpi.

This is a simple graphic obtained by making a screen capture of a monitor's background, importing it into PageMaker, cropped, and enlarged.

Here is how to make and use a screen capture:

1. Make sure that the screen displays exactly what you want to capture and that the Pointer is not in the picture, unless you want it to be in the captured image.

2. If you want to capture the entire screen, press the Print Screen key on your keyboard. On most computers if you just want to capture the active dialog or window, press Alt+Print Screen or Alt+Shift+Print Screen. When you do this the current screen is copied to the Clipboard. (Note that the image is not saved to disk and only exists in the Clipboard. If you are not going to immediately use the image, run the Clipboard Viewer located in the Main group and choose Save from the File menu.)

3. Use Paste in PageMaker's Edit menu to put the image into your publication.

4. After the screen capture has been placed, it can be sized, cropped, rotated, or otherwise transformed in PageMaker.

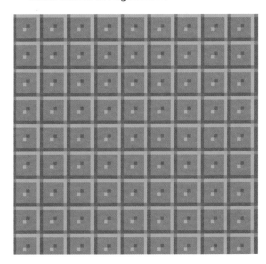

This is the same screen capture as shown below left, resized, and uncropped.

Again, this is the same screen capture, cropped, stretched, and resized.

To be used in PageMaker documents, graphics must be converted to electronic format. This can be done in several ways. They can be scanned, drawn in a graphics program, or traced and redrawn. This section will explore these different methods.

Scanning

There are many different types of scanners, ranging from small, hand-held units to large drum models. Their workings are similar to those of photocopiers, but the images they capture are translated into data files for electronic display and output.

As always, the type of publication you're producing will dictate which kind of scanner you employ for converting your graphics to electronic format. For a document reproduced from laser prints, it is not necessary to use a scanner with resolution higher than 300 SPI. (While it is common to use DPI to indicate the resolution of a scanner, it is not accurate. A scanner actually examines samples, not dots while it scans.)

Service bureaus often provide flatbed, slide/ transparency, and drum scanning services, though at a relatively high cost. (You can expect these costs to drop as low-cost Photo CD technology becomes more widely available.)

■ Handheld scanners

Handheld scanners are inexpensive and are great for capturing images to be used as templates for redrawing in Illustrator or FreeHand. Some have resolution as high as 400 SPI, and support 256 levels of gray. One problem with handheld scanners is that you need to combine several scans of one image to create a full page.

■ Flatbed scanners

With these scanners you lay a piece of art—a photograph, drawing, or other image—directly on a glass, close the lid, and scan. They can be either black and white or color, and their resolution ranges from 300 SPI to 600 SPI. Black and white flatbed scanners support up to 256 levels of gray, completely acceptable for PageMaker projects.

One of my favorite things to do with flatbed scanners is scan 3-D objects. You can use anything—tools, hands, crumpled paper, flowers—and get some great scans with shadows and texture. You need to creatively drape the object to block light, because the top probably won't close. Two cautions: be careful not to scratch the glass on the flatbed scanner; never look into a scanner to scan your face.

■ Slide/transparency scanners

If the photographs for your publication are slides, you can have them scanned on a slide scanner. Scanned slides produce a great image, as long as the scanner which is being used has been recently calibrated, and the operator is knowledgeable. Larger transparencies also can be scanned, and produce even better results because there can be higher resolution—since the image is larger than a slide and enables the scan to contain more data.

■ Drum scanners

On these scanners, art is attached to a drum that rotates rapidly and is scanned at very accurate, very high resolution. These scanners are found in service bureaus and prepress companies.

Scanning resolution

Resolution is determined in samples per inch, (SPI) and the higher your resolution, the sharper your image. When art is scanned, it must be at a SPI two times the intended line screen of the halftone. That means if you are going to print at a line screen of 133 (metal plates, mid- to high-quality printing) you will need scans at 266 SPI. Of course, this formula changes if you intend to reduce or enlarge the scan once it's placed on the page. If you'll be using it at 50% its original size, scan at 133 SPI for a 133 line screen. If you'll be using it at twice its size, you'll need a scan of 532 SPI. These are just guidelines. If you are unsure how large you'll be using a particular image, scan at higher resolution; if you don't need it the only consequence is that the file will contain more information than it needs and will print more slowly.

The TIFF scan above is assigned 53 lines per inch in Image Control. The same scan below has been assigned a 133 LPI screen.

Graphics software

Many different graphics programs can be used to produce, retouch, and prepare art for electronic publication in PageMaker. Each program serves specific purposes, and it is beyond the scope of this book to examine them in detail. They can be used alone or in conjunction with each other to produce graphics.

Once you have created a file in any of these programs, saved it in a format PageMaker can accept, and import it into your publication. Color information assigned in the graphic program will be maintained in PageMaker and can be separated to film for process or spot color reproduction when the PageMaker file is output to film.

Some typical graphics programs that can be used with PageMaker (and there are others) are listed below:

■ **Drawing**
  Aldus FreeHand
  Adobe Illustrator
  Micrografx Designer
  Corel Draw

■ **3-D**
  3D Studio

■ **Paint**
  Adobe Photoshop
  Fractal Painter
  Micrografx Picture Publisher
  Aldus PhotoStyler

Scans for tracing

Often, a quick sketch of something is scanned and imported as a template into Aldus FreeHand, Adobe Illustrator, or a similar program to be traced. In object-oriented drawing programs like these, you can achieve precise line weights, fills, and colors that would require unusually well-developed drawing skills and the finest art tools if created by hand.

Once the tracing is completed, delete the scan itself, leaving the new drawing in the file. You should, generally, save the drawing as an Encapsulated PostScript (EPS) file. It can then be placed into a PageMaker document as a graphic.

Acceptable file formats

After creating work in graphics software for use in PageMaker, you must save your file in a format PageMaker can accept. Here are some recommendations for specific software programs:

Adobe Illustrator	EPS
Aldus FreeHand	EPS
Aldus Persuasion	WMF(PC), PICT(Mac)
Aldus TableEditor	WMF
Arts & Letters 3.01	EPS, TIFF
AutoCad 9.1	EPS
CorelDRAW!	EPS, TIFF
AutoCAD	DXF
Excel Charts	WMF, XLC
Excel Spreadsheets	XLS
Harvard Graphics	EPS
HPGraphicsGallery	TIFF
Lotus Freelance Graphics	EPS, TIFF
MacPaint	PNT
Micrografx Designer	TIFF
PC Paintbrush	TIFF
Publishers Paintbrush	PCX
TIFF files	TIFF
Windows Paintbrush 3.0	BMP, PCX

Other supported graphic formats

BMP, DCS, PCX, PhotoCD(PCD), PNT, TIF, CMYK TIFF

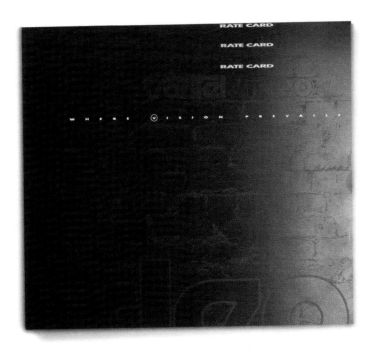

This rate card uses a photograph of a distinctive brick wall from the client's building. The photograph was scanned, posterized, and lightened, to serve as a graphic pattern.
Designer: Mike Bertoni, PRINTZ Electronic Design, San Francisco
Client: Varitel Video

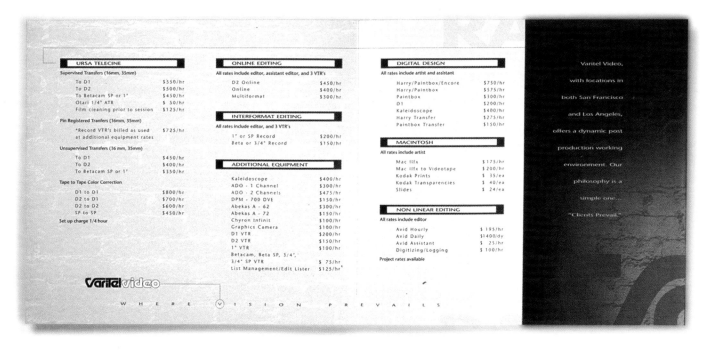

URSA TELECINE

Supervised Transfers (16mm, 35mm)

To D1	$550/hr
To D2	$500/hr
To Betacam SP or 1"	$450/hr
Otari 1/4" ATR	$ 50/hr
Film cleaning prior to session	$125/hr

Pin Registered Tranfers (16mm, 35mm)

*Record VTR's billed as used at additional equipment rates	$725/hr

Unsupervised Transfers (16 mm, 35mm)

To D1	$450/hr
To D2	$400/hr
To Betacam SP or 1"	$350/hr

Tape to Tape Color Correction

D1 to D1	$800/hr
D2 to D1	$700/hr
D2 to D2	$600/hr
SP to SP	$450/hr

Set up charge 1/4 hour

ONLINE EDITING

All rates include editor, assistant editor, and 3 VTR's

D2 Online	$450/hr
Online	$400/hr
Multiformat	$300/hr

INTERFORMAT EDITING

All rates include editor, and 3 VTR's

1" or SP Record	$200/hr
Beta or 3/4" Record	$150/hr

ADDITIONAL EQUIPMENT

Kaleidoscope	$400/hr
ADO - 1 Channel	$300/hr
ADO - 2 Channels	$475/hr
DPM - 700 DVE	$150/hr
Abekas A - 62	$300/hr
Abekas A - 72	$150/hr
Chyron Infinit	$100/hr
Graphics Camera	$100/hr
D1 VTR	$200/hr
D2 VTR	$150/hr
1" VTR	$100/hr
Betacam, Beta SP, 3/4", 3/4" SP VTR	$ 75/hr
List Management/Edit Lister	$125/hr

DIGITAL DESIGN

All rates include artist and assistant

Harry/Paintbox/Encore	$750/hr
Harry/Paintbox	$575/hr
Paintbox	$300/hr
D1	$200/hr
Kaleidoscope	$400/hr
Harry Transfer	$275/hr
Paintbox Transfer	$150/hr

MACINTOSH

All rates include artist

Mac IIfx	$175/hr
Mac IIfx to Videotape	$200/hr
Kodak Prints	$ 35/ea
Kodak Transparencies	$ 40/ea
Slides	$ 24/ea

NON LINEAR EDITING

All rates include editor

Avid Hourly	$ 195/hr
Avid Daily	$1400/dy
Avid Assistant	$ 25/hr
Digitizing/Logging	$ 100/hr

Project rates available

Varitel Video, with locations in both San Francisco and Los Angeles, offers a dynamic post production working environment. Our philosophy is a simple one... "Clients Prevail."

Varitelvideo

W H E R E   V I S I O N   P R E V A I L S

After you have converted graphics to an electronic file format, they can be imported into PageMaker. There are different ways of doing this, and choices must be made based on how the graphic will be updated, and where the information it contains is stored.

Draw- and paint-type graphics

The graphics that PageMaker is able to import fall into two categories: Draw-type (object-oriented) graphics, and Paint-type (bitmapped) images. Draw-type images use mathematical equations to describe the paths of lines and fills; therefore, they can be re-sized once in PageMaker with no degradation of quality. Paint-type images, which are drawings created in paint programs or scans, are resolution-dependent and their quality can deteriorate as they are sized larger. Both draw- and paint-type graphics can be imported into PageMaker similarly.

Formats PageMaker imports

TIFF, BMP, PCX, EPS, MacPaint, WMF, and PICT formats can all be imported by Page-Maker. You can see a complete list of the program's Windows-compatible formats by choosing on-line Help, and viewing the Filters on-line tip. Help is found under the Windows menu.

If your graphics software can save a file in one of these formats, graphics you create can be used in PageMaker. If not, you may need a graphics conversion program to change your image into one of these formats. This may also be true if you wish to import a draw-type graphic created on a Mac into PageMaker for the PC. Some conversion programs include HotShot Graphics by SymSoft, HiJaak by Inset Systems, or The GraphicsLink Plus+ by Harvard Graphics.

Placing graphics

Placing graphics is executed with Page-Maker's Place command, found under the File menu. This method of importing a graphic enables you to create a link to the original source file—meaning that the file information does not need to be included in your PageMaker document, and that the graphic can be updated automatically if the source file changes.

Pasting graphics

This method of importing graphics uses the Windows Clipboard. You can Copy the graphic with the source program open, then open your PageMaker document and Paste. This method does not however, allow for graphics to be linked to their original source.

OLE (Object linking and embedding)

This is a convention for sharing information between programs. It works by letting you build a link between the OLE-aware program in which the object was created (the source) and the program into which you paste it (the destination). To paste an OLE link, save your file in the source program, and then copy what you want to paste into PageMaker. Once you are in PageMaker, choose Paste special from the Edit menu, and click on Paste link in the dialog box.

External linking

When you import graphic files larger than a specified preference setting, you see an alert message which asks if you want to store a complete copy of the graphic in the publication. If you choose not to do so, PageMaker will import a low-resolution version of the graphic for display purposes only, and establishes a link to the original graphic. You must ensure that you maintain the link for proper printed output. If not, the low-res display graphic will be substituted, even with high resolution imagesetting.

Automatic link updating

When a graphic is placed, PageMaker establishes a link to the original document on your hard drive. You can choose for the graphic to be automatically updated if the source file is changed. To set this default:

1. Make sure PageMaker is active with no publication open.

2. Under the Element menu, open Link options....

3. Check the box to Update automatically. Click on the OK button.

4. Each time you open your PageMaker publication, it will check the source graphic to see if it has been changed. If so, it will update the graphic with the new version.

Library palette

Using the library palette is an easy way to import and organize collections of frequently used text and graphics. You can categorize and search for objects by key words, display names, and thumbnail images.

Adding objects to the Library is easy. Select the object, open Library from the Windows menu, and click the add (+) button. All link information about the object is retained and added to the Library.

Inline graphics

When you want a graphic to remain with specific text, it can be placed as an inline graphic. Inline graphics can be used only when the graphic will fit entirely within the flowed text block.

To import a graphic as part of a text block (or "inline"), place the cursor in the text where you wish to insert the graphic. Use the Place or Paste command, and the graphic will become part of the text block. You can also copy or cut an existing graphic from the page and paste it into the text.

It is not possible to flow several lines of text around an inline graphic; instead, when the graphic is imported, it becomes a "character" in a line and has auto leading characteristics based on its size. The graphic takes its spacing cues from the surrounding text. It's often necessary to adjust the leading or spacing of an inline graphic. Here's how to do it:

1. To adjust leading, select the paragraph which includes the graphic. Open the Type specifications dialog box (Control-T) and change the leading to whatever value you have used for all the text in the text block.

2. To move the graphic vertically, use the Pointer tool in Layout view. Point to the graphic and click the mouse button. The graphic can then be moved up or down by moving the mouse.

3. To adjust the distance from the graphic to text that precedes or follows it, place the cursor between the graphic and text and use the space bar to insert spaces, or kern space by pressing Control-Backspace (to move text closer) or Control-Shift-Backspace to move it farther away.

The text block below shows a scan used twice as an inline graphic. On the facing page you can see how the graphics are displayed when the same text block is opened in Story Editor—as a simple rectangle.

Lorem ipsum dolor sit amet, consectetuer adipiscing elit, sed diam nonummy nibh euismod tincidunt. Ut laoreet dolore magna aliquam erat volutpat.

Ut wisi enim ad minim veniam, quis nostrud exerci. Tation ullamcorper suscipit lobortis nisl ut aliquip

Normal	▨ Lorem ipsum dolor sit amet, consectetuer adipiscing elit, sed diam nonum euismod tincidunt. Ut laoreet do-lore magna aliquam erat volutpat.
Normal	
Normal	▨ Ut wisi enim ad minim veniam, quis nostrud exerci. Tation ullamcorper su lobortis nisl ut aliquip

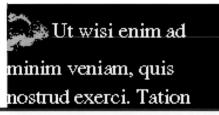

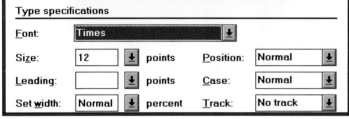

Type specifications

Font:	Times		
Size:	12	points	**P**osition: Normal
Leading:		points	**C**ase: Normal
Set **w**idth:	Normal	percent	**T**rack: No track

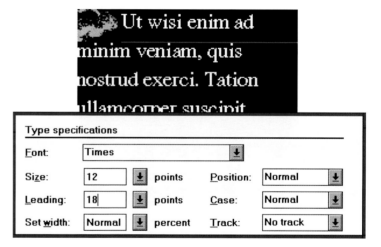

Type specifications

Font:	Times		
Size:	12	points	**P**osition: Normal
Leading:	18	points	**C**ase: Normal
Set **w**idth:	Normal	percent	**T**rack: No track

The leading of inline graphics can be tricky. On the left, you can see that the first line containing the graphic has different leading from the rest of the text block. This can be solved by selecting the entire text block, and specifying a leading value that can accommodate the size of the graphic. You can use the pointer tool and move the graphic up or down to further adjust its placement.

Finding, creating, and importing the right graphics for your publication is just the beginning. You must make the most of your graphics when you place them onto the page. There are many ways to use graphics very effectively.

The photograph used on the cover of this brochure is featured prominently because it is so dramatic.
Design by: The Newsletter Company, Campbell, CA
Client: Wearnes Technology Corporation

Feature graphics prominently

If the graphic is very strong or colorful, or if it conveys vital information, it should be treated as a stand-alone element. Type should not be printed on top of the graphic, nor should the graphic be small. Instead, feature it prominently and consider a bleed off the page, placement across two pages, callouts or captions pointing to the graphic, or other methods of drawing attention to it.

Integrate graphics with text wrap

Text wrap is a good way to integrate a prominent graphic into a page. Here's how to work with PageMaker's text wrap feature:

1. Arrange the text on your page, and import the graphic by using the "Place" command under File.

2. Place the graphic on top of the text which will wrap around it. While the graphic is selected, choose Text wrap... from the Element menu.

3. You have two Wrap options from which to choose when the object is first placed: wrap and no wrap. Choose wrap by clicking on the middle box. Now, the three different wrapping options appear. The first one causes text to stop flowing above the graphic, the second causes it to stop at the top of the graphic and continue below it, and the third causes it be repelled on all sides of the graphic. You set the distance the text wraps from the graphic in the Standoff boxes when you click OK.

4. Your graphic is now surrounded by a dotted line that defines the area where text will not flow. If you click and drag on one of these lines, it can be moved farther away from the graphic, or even inside the boundaries of the graphic (if you want text to print on the graphic). If you click once on a line and release the mouse button, you break the line and insert a new point in it. These points can be created and moved around to define how the text will wrap around the graphic.

5. Pay attention to how the type can be affected by the text wrap. Don't allow several lines of narrow columns with just one word. It's better not to use text wrap than to create ugly or difficult to read type just for the sake of a wrap. Resizing the graphic slightly by holding the Shift key and moving one of the graphic's handles (as opposed to the boundary's handles) changes the flow of the text.

Use graphics under text

If your photograph or image is not particularly strong on its own, it may look better placed under the text. Use caution when taking this approach, however, because text can be difficult to read with a strong or distracting graphic behind it. (This is a particular risk when you are printing in only one color.)

Use color whenever possible

If you are using a second color in your publication, you may wish to include that color in your graphics, even if they are originally black and white line art or gray-scale images. Gray-scale photographs and drawings have tonal variation. Your second color will appear in many different levels, giving added impact to the document.

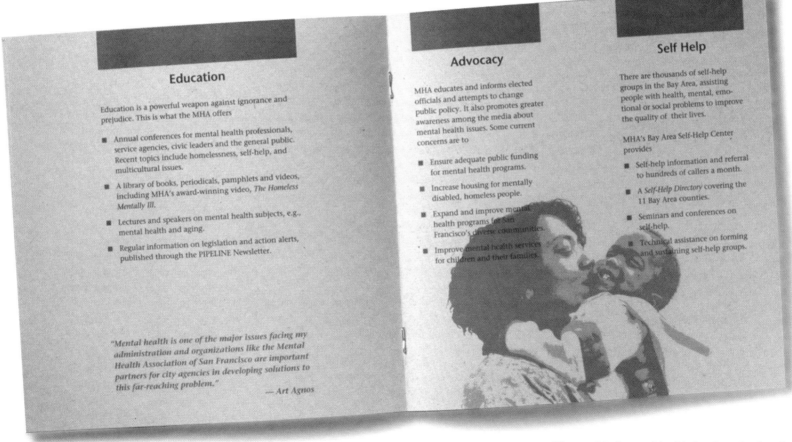

The graphic featured in this brochure is placed behind the text.
Designer: Michael J. Nolan
Client: San Francisco Mental Health Association

Backgrounds are patterns, textures, or other images that lie beneath the text and graphics of a page. They add pleasing depth and interest to any printed piece.

Sources for backgrounds

There are many creative options for backgrounds. One designer I know took photographs of the concrete walls in a parking garage and then scanned them to create an effective background. I once used lace from a bridal veil with black paper behind it on a flatbed scanner to create a background for a wedding invitation. Sheets of wrapping paper, or even imported book papers found in art supply stores also make good sources for backgrounds.

Backgrounds can be created with a scanner, or drawn in a graphics or paint program.

Background intensity

If scans are used as backgrounds with type placed over them, ensure that they are not too strong; otherwise, the type is hard to read. If you are printing in one color, the background must be even more subdued. The Image Control feature in PageMaker allows you to lighten TIFF scans used as backgrounds. (See page 150.) Because laser prints do not give an accurate indication of the darkness of a screen, you should run a paper imagesetter test to study the contrast between the background and the type overlaying it.

Sometimes backgrounds are a solid color, a screened color, or a gradation of color. It is important to judge how readable text will be in these situations as well. For proofing purposes, it is best to use a high-resolution system, because a laser printer will not print accurate levels of contrast.

Other backgrounds

Even if you don't have access to a scanner or an illustration program, you can still create backgrounds for your documents. Use PageMaker's graphics tools to create rectangles, squares, circles, or ellipses, and overlay them with lines or other patterns found within the program. Or, take a more conventional route and have your printer strip in photographs or even photocopies that you provide. Because this will eliminate some of your control, be sure to see a blueline (a composite proof made from film negatives) and perhaps a press check (examination of the first few printed pieces before the entire run is printed), to ensure that the background isn't too strong.

The graphics shown here were made by scanning a doily and some dried flowers.

The brochure shown on the left uses a background pattern created in Adobe Illustrator, and saved as an EPS file. The letterhead on the right was created with TIFF scans placed over one another.
Designer: Carol Kappel, Pearson, Crahan & Fletcher, Indianapolis
Client: St. Vincent's Hospital

There are two kinds of backgrounds in the St. Vincent's Hospital material. The letterhead from the Breast Center uses scans, while the annual report contains PostScript patterns drawn in another program.

The following steps show how to create a page similar to the letterhead, using backgrounds of gray-scale scans and spot color printing. (This applies only to TIFF format files, which can be lightened with PageMaker's Image Control feature.)

1. Set up an 8 ½" x 11" page with 0 margins on all sides. This enables you to see the edge of the page with guidelines displayed after the scans have been added.

2. Make sure guidelines are set to Front in the Preferences dialog box (now found under the File menu rather than its former location under Edit in earlier PageMaker versions), so you can measure where to crop the image.

3. Place the TIFF scan that serves as the bottom layer on your page by using the Place command from the File menu.

4. Use the Pointer tool on one of the handles of the selected image and hold the Shift key to restrain the proportions of the image as you drag and enlarge it to fill the page. The first scan placed must extend 1/4" beyond the page on all sides.

5. Select the scan, copy it, and "power paste" (Control Shift P) to place the copy exactly on top of the original.

6. Open Image Control, and use the lightness control arrows to lighten the second scan—enough for type to be readable over the scan. (You should run a test file on a high-resolution printer to make sure the lightness is correct.)

7. Use the Cropping tool on the corners and crop the top scan to measurement lines an equal distance in from the edge of the page on all sides. (You may wish to crop in a bit more from the bottom for better framing.)

8. Place the type you'll be using on top of the lighter scan, and choose another color—if you are printing two-color.

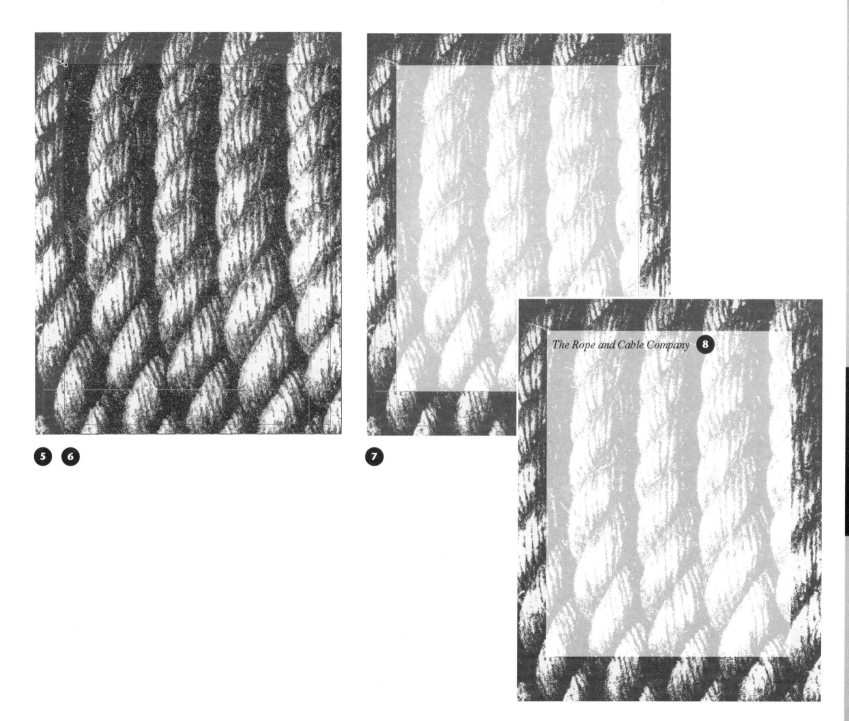

The Rope and Cable Company 8

5 6 7

Borders are an effective way to frame a graphic, pull quote, photograph, or full page—if they are used with restraint and purpose. A good border complements the message of the publication.

Use discretion when creating borders. Some users of PageMaker fall prey to "border-mania," using combinations of drop shadows, double or triple rules, and rounded corner boxes on the same page.

Here are some simple ideas for creating borders that avoid the clichés:

A drop shadow border

This drop shadow is soft and natural in its gradation. You may need to experiment a few times to get it right.

1. Create a rectangle or rounded corner box with a paper fill.

2. Copy the figure (Control-C).

3. "Power paste" (Control-Shift-P) the figure.

4. Using the control panel, move the new figure in very small increments (a point or two) down and to the right.

5. "Power paste" several more figures. (They should paste offset by the same distance as the first figure was moved.)

6. Select the first copied figure, and change its fill to 90% screen. Send it to the back (Control-B).

7. Continue with the succeeding figures, changing fills to the next lower screen value, and sending each one to the back. The bottom layer should have a 10% screen.

A line border

This simple border can be created in seconds. Additional layers in different colors give it even more interest.

1. Create two rectangles of different sizes, select a line pattern from the Fill menu for the larger one and give the smaller one paper fill.

2. Choose a second color from the color palette.

3. Place the smaller rectangle on top of the larger one using the Bring to front command from the Edit menu, and measure the distance from the edge on all sides to make sure it's correct. (Do this at 200% or 400% view, but don't try to count the lines for measurement because their number changes in each view).

A dingbat border

Explore the variety of dingbat characters in WingDings by running the Character Map applet in the Accessories group, changing the font to WingDings and looking at the characters. You can combine one or more characters to create a border such as this one:

1. Create a text block, and type into it the dingbat characters desired for the border.

2. Select the type, and use the Force Justify… command under Alignment.

3. Copy the text block and "Power Paste" (Control-Shift-P) over it.

4. While the pasted object is selected, using text rotation, rotate it 180° and move it down in place for the bottom border.

5. Create a text block of the appropriate length for the sides, adding the proper number of characters.

6. Copy that text block, "power paste", and rotate it using the Control palette or Rotation tool into the proper position for the other side.

7. Use the Box tool, and choose appropriate line weights and colors to surround the dingbats. View at 400% to ensure measurements are accurate.

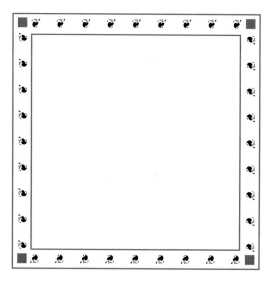

Charts and graphs

Charts and graphs are a very effective way to summarize numerical data and tell a visual story. They take many forms, from pie charts to bar graphs. Many spreadsheet programs have the capability to create graphics from the data that has been entered. If you have a program like this, it is efficient to build your chart or graph in that program and import it into PageMaker.

Importing spreadsheets

There are several methods of importing charts and graphs into PageMaker, including Place, and Paste link. Before styling your graphic in the spreadsheet program, be certain that you are using fonts and colors that will look good in your document, because once placed into your PageMaker publication, they can only be changed using the source program. You may want to create headings or other labels in PageMaker, to have more immediate control over how they look in your publication.

When a chart or graph is imported from a spreadsheet program, it will be treated as a graphic, which means you can enlarge/reduce, crop, stretch, rotate or otherwise manipulate it, but cannot edit it.

Basic graphs created in PageMaker

If you do not have a spreadsheet program capable of building a chart or graph, you can use the graphics tools in PageMaker to do so. Here's a simple process for building a bar graph (the measurements are arbitrary; you can use your own):

1. Draw a one point horizontal line 3 inches long, and place an 8 point 0, right aligned, numeral in a small text block to the left of the line.

2. Copy the line and the text block next to it and choose Multiple paste from the Edit menu. For the distance, choose .2 inches for vertical offset 0 for horizontal offset, and paste 10 copies. This will yield 11 lines, evenly spaced .2 inches apart.

3. Beginning with the second text block from the bottom, click into the block, choose Select all, and retype 10. Do the same and enter 20 for the next one, 30 for the one after that, and so forth, until the top line is labeled 100.

4. Create a rectangle that is .2 inches wide and extends from the 0 line to just above the 50 line. It should have a 20% fill and no lines.

5. Copy the rectangle and multiple paste it six times with a vertical offset measurement of .4 inch and horizontal offset of 0.

6. Use the middle handle on the top of each rectangle to adjust its height—35 percent would be midway between the 30 and 40 line. These adjustments will be by eye, and it should be fairly easy to make them look accurate.

7. You can "decorate" the graph any way you want, but the basic principle should be to keep it simple.

Another way to create the same type of graph is to make the lines and labels one text block using tabs and leaders (see page 96). This enables you to change the type specifications for everything at once. You can also use paragraph rules instead of leader tabs for great control over line styles.

Simple graphs such as the one below, can be made quickly using PageMaker's Multiple paste… feature by following the steps outlined here.

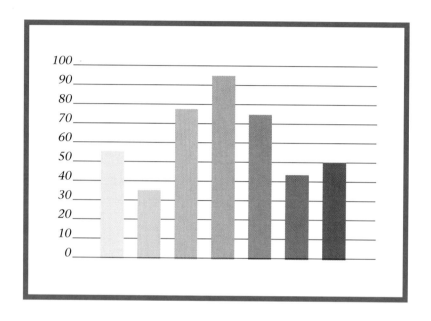

Logos

Whether you are designing a new logo, or using an existing one, logo treatments are not something to be taken lightly. Ideally, an organization's logo will be used for years, or even decades, so it should seldom, if ever, be changed. This way, it builds equity—public recognition. Versatility is important too, because a logo needs to be effective in all sizes, from the smallest ad to billboards and the sides of trucks.

Designing logos

In your work, you may be called upon to design a logo. There are many things to keep in mind as you embark upon a logo assignment:

■ Design for all sizes

Avoid fine lines and intricate illustrations, because they may become obscure when the logo is printed very small, such as on a business card. Pay special attention to any reversed type.

■ Design for all uses

A logo must have the same impact whether it's used in an advertisement or to identify a building. Plan for other uses even if you're designing a company logo for a PageMaker newsletter. This means you should make the logo bold and distinctive. It also means that it should look as good in black and white as it does in color.

■ Keep it simple

Complicated color blends, special inks, obscure fonts—all these can make it difficult for your client to reprint letterhead or other materials. You may not be available to guide the client in the future applications of the logo.

■ Avoid trendiness

To ensure that a logo has staying power, avoid using trendy colors or typefaces. Those that have appeal today could look hopelessly dated in just a few years. Strong, primary colors are a good bet, and classic typefaces not only ensure readability, but also lend an air of solidity to the logo.

■ Make it proportional

A logo should not be noticeably horizontal or vertical, because that may restrict its uses. For example, if a long horizontal logo needs to be placed into a tall, thin advertisement, it will need to be sized smaller to keep its proportions. See if it fits into a circle or square. This is a good test for proper proportions. As a rule of thumb, don't exceed a 1:2 ratio in either direction (twice as wide as tall, or twice as tall as wide).

Design as a unit

When logos are created in a graphics program they can be exported as a single piece. Programs such as Aldus FreeHand or Adobe Illustrator are ideal for creating logos. This allows for easy resizing in page layout applications, and avoids such problems as point size in relation to graphic elements and letter spacing.

Typographical treatments

If a client does not wish to use a graphic, you can still create a distinctive typographical logo. It is very important to pay attention to kerning, line spacing, and other typographical concerns. Try to create such a logo in a program other than PageMaker if possible.

Build upon equity

If you are designing a new logo, try to use elements of the old one to establish continuity.

Using existing logos

Organizations are understandably concerned about their logos and how they are used. As a designer, you must never take liberties with your client's identity.

Ask for a style manual

If you're doing work for a large company, they probably have a corporate style manual that will tell you the appropriate use of their logo. It will also contain the proper PMS colors.

Don't crowd the logo

Design your page so the logo stands alone, surrounded by plenty of white space. Make sure it's appropriately large relative to other visual elements on the page.

Don't use the logo as a graphic

Resist the temptation to use the company's logo as a screened background with text on top of it. Similarly, don't use the logo as part of some other graphic, such as superimposed over a photograph. Always treat it as a stand-alone element.

Never redraw a logo

Don't redraw a company's logo or reset it in type, no matter how simple it may look. There may be subtle nuances you are not aware of, and it will only cause your client distress if you miss them. Instead, ask for a photostat or electronic file of the logo. If unavailable, ask the client to carefully review your re-created version of the logo.

Use the logo as a starting point

If the logo will be featured prominently in your design, you can use its colors, typefaces, and other forms as elements in your publication. This will lend an air of cohesiveness to your document.

Transforming

After locating, converting, and importing graphics, they can be transformed to polish their appearance. PageMaker enables you to resize, stretch, crop, skew, rotate, and reflect graphics with ease and control.

Cropping graphics

Imported graphics sometimes need to be cropped to eliminate areas you don't want to print. To reduce the size of graphic files, you can crop images in the application in which they were created.

If you cannot crop in the original program, you can use the Cropping tool in PageMaker. Here are some points to remember:

■ Objects can only be cropped at right angles; to crop on a diagonal, position a paper filled rectangle over the image and rotate the rectangle appropriately.

■ If you want to crop something from the middle of a photo or line art, you can possibly use one or more polygons with different percentage screen fills. Go to a 400% size view to position these polygons accurately.

■ To save time and eliminate unnecessary keystrokes, always use a corner handle when cropping; this way, you change two measurements at once.

■ To replace a previously cropped image with a newer or corrected version without cropping the replacement image, select the graphic you wish to replace, and choose Replace entire graphic under the Place option in the File menu. Unless the size or proportions of the graphic have been altered, the new image will come in with the correct cropping information.

Crop effectively

Prominently featuring part of a photo or illustration is often more effective than using the entire photo. Decide what is in the graphic that contains the most important information or will prove most enticing to the reader, and crop out the rest. Here's how to crop a photo or graphic:

1. Choose the Cropping tool in the Toolbox.

2. Select the graphic to be cropped by positioning the Cropping tool over it and clicking.

3. Move the Cropping tool so that a handle of the graphic appears inside the "sights" of the tool. (You can crop two directions at once by using one of the corner handles; this can save time and keystrokes.)

4. Hold down the mouse button until the Cropping tool changes to a two-headed arrow. Then move the mouse in the direction you wish to crop.

5. After you have the correct proportions for the image, you can click on the center of it, and turn the Cropping tool to a Grabber hand which moves the image around inside the borders of the crop as you move the mouse.

6. If you change the original graphic in another program and wish to replace an earlier cropped and sized version, select the graphic to be replaced with the Pointer tool before executing the Place command under File menu. Identify the file name for the altered graphic, and click the replace entire graphic button in the dialog box. The sizing and cropping information remain the same.

Resizing graphics

To ensure that a graphic retains its original proportions during resizing, hold the Shift key down when moving a handle. In addition, keep these things in mind when resizing a graphic:

■ If part of the graphic is already aligned correctly (e.g., a left top corner of the graphic fit in the left top corner of a column), use the handle opposite (in this case, the right bottom corner) to resize the graphic, so you won't have to realign it.

■ If a scan is to be significantly reduced in size from the original placed file, consider reducing it in the program that created it. (For example, reducing an image size in Aldus PhotoStyler or Adobe Photoshop will significantly decrease file size, making imagesetting faster.)

■ If a scan is going to be increased dramatically in size, you may end up with a blurred, highly-pixellated image with poor resolution. There is nothing you can do if an image began small, or a scan's file size was reduced. In this case, you should not use the graphic in any size greater than 150% of its original size.

■ When it is important to keep the proportions while resizing a rectangle drawn in PageMaker, it's almost automatic that you'll hold the shift key and watch your rectangle become a square when you click on one of its handles. Using the Control palette instead is the easiest way to resize a rectangle. (See Control Palette, page 62.)

The self-promotion piece to the left shows the use of many different graphic elements, some of which have been transformed by stretching, skewing, and rotating.
Design by: Bay Graphics, Berkeley, CA

143

Distort the image

PageMaker's features enable you to distort and manipulate images. Stretched, rotated, reflected, and distorted images give a modern look to your publication—probably because they draw attention to the fact that a computer was used in its creation. In addition to giving an interesting look to good graphics, distortion can be used to compensate for low-quality original artwork.

Here are some ways to give graphics a distorted, abstract appearance:

- Stretch the image until pixellation becomes obvious.

- Stretch more in one direction than another. This works best if the stretch is so dramatic as to be very obvious.

- Stretch, and rotate or reflect the graphic.

- Increase contrast dramatically in Image Control to posterize images. (This only works on black and white, paint-type, and gray-scale TIFF images.)

- Print the graphic in a second color, perhaps as a negative image.

- Copy and "power paste" (Control-Shift-P) a graphic over itself. Crop away part of the top layer. Use Image control… to make it a negative, or use another color to make it different from the rest of the graphic.

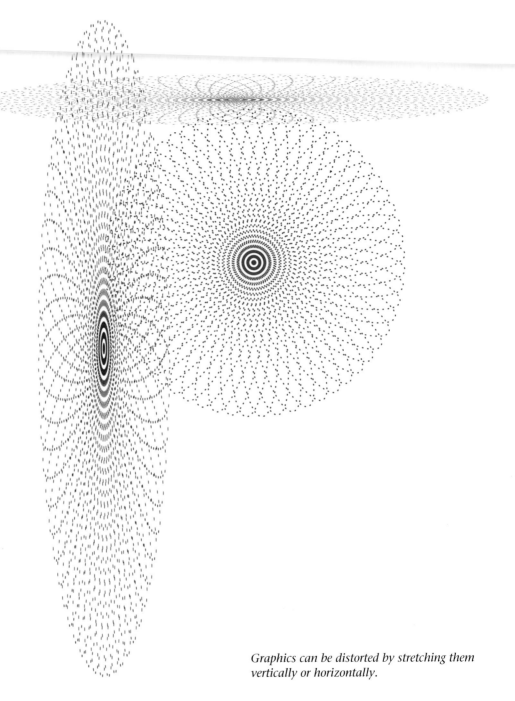

Graphics can be distorted by stretching them vertically or horizontally.

The brochure cover shown here uses obvious pixellation in a scanned photograph of sky and clouds to emphasize the computerized aspect of the company's design services.
Designer: Mike Bertoni
Client: PRINTZ Electronic Design, San Francisco

Image control...

Image control is used to change the appearance or printing characteristics of paint-type and gray-scale TIFF images. (It does not work with color TIFF files.) You can use Image control on any imported TIFF file without worry, because if you make choices which you later decide are wrong, you can click Reset to revert to the previous settings.

You can print an image as a gray-scale, halftone with dots, or a line pattern. If you choose to print it as a halftone, you can indicate the frequency of dots—dictated by the printing method being used, and if you're using a line screen for special effects, you can choose the angle of the lines.

Image control for special effects

If your project is to be printed in one or two colors only, you can achieve a wide range of effects using this tool.

■ Increase the contrast to reduce the number of levels of gray. This will posterize any image, reducing it to its essential information.

■ Use a coarse line screen, or change the angle of the line screen to abstract an image.

■ Lighten the image so that it can be printed under text or other graphics.

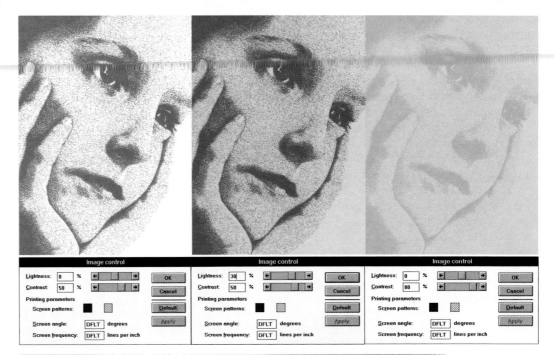

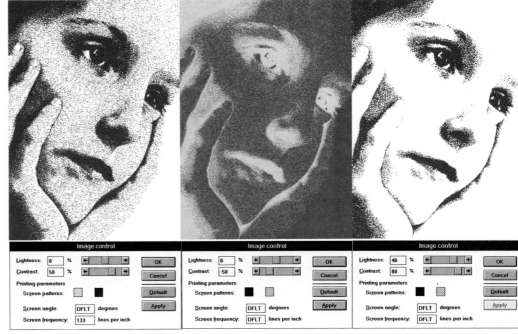

Setting line screens

Image control is used on TIFF images to assign the correct line screen for optimal reproduction, before your document is sent for high-resolution imagesetting. This is accomplished with individual images placed into your file—or new to PageMaker 5.0, this can be done globally when you print. If you want to run your whole job at a particular line screen, choose Print, click the Color button, and enter the LPI in the Ruling entry field. Regardless of what resolution your image was scanned and saved at, you must still assign a line screen value if you are going to print it as a halftone. Not assigning one risks that the image will be set at a coarser line screen than is desirable.

- If you are using a photocopier for your final duplication, you want to assign no more than an 85 line screen.

- If you are using offset printing for your final duplication and your printer is using paper plates rather than metal plates, set the line screen at no more than 120 LPI.

- If your printer is using metal plates for high quality offset printing, choose a line screen of 133 to 150 (or higher, if your printer is capable of the highest quality).

- Always include the line screen as part of the file information with any order you place to a service bureau for high-resolution imagesetting.

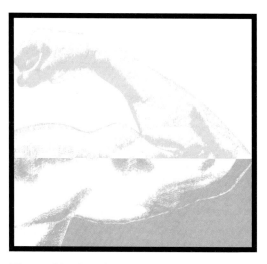

The graphic above is created by placing a TIFF scan, copying it, and "power pasting" (Control-Shift-P) it exactly on top of itself. Next, use Image control… to create a negative image of the top copy and crop down to reveal part of the original graphic underneath.

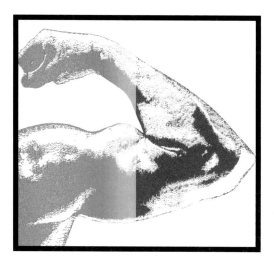

This graphic uses the same principles outlined above, but each scan is printed in a different color rather than as a positive or negative.

Creating keylines

It's very useful to have the capability to draw a line around, or place a background behind a graphic quickly and precisely, as you can do with the Create keyline... Aldus Addition. This new addition simplifies the task, and allows for accuracy not previously available.

For Create keyline... to work best, it is important to perform your photo cropping, sizing, rotation, and skewing before applying the Addition. Otherwise, you must perform these functions separately on the graphic and the keyline.

1. Select the graphic you wish to keyline. In the example here, a gray-scale TIFF scan was changed to black and white in Image control... so that it would become transparent, allowing the red background to show through.

2. Choose Create keyline... from Aldus Additions under the Utilities menu.

3. Indicate the number of points you want the keyline to be outside the graphic in the dialog box. If you want it to be flush with the edge of the graphic, choose 0. This example extends the keyline 1.0 point on all sides.

4. Indicate whether the keyline is to be behind or in front of the graphic.

5. Select Attributes to specify background color, line weight, and color.

6. Click the OK button and the Addition does the rest.

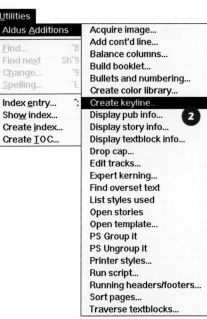

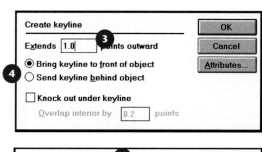

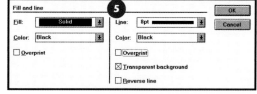

The photo of the earth as seen on this holiday
card, was transformed by using the Lighten
feature in Image control.... A gradient fill goes
from full-strength blue to white on the inside
of the card.
Designer: Michael J. Nolan
Client: Film & Video Service, San Francisco

Gradient fills

Gradient fills imitate nature's light as found in sunsets and shadows, and add depth and drama to your publication. You cannot create gradient fills in PageMaker, but they are covered here because they are often taken from other sources and incorporated into PageMaker documents.

Uses for gradient fills

Because of the ease of creating them in electronic publishing programs, gradient fills have become very popular—almost to the point of overuse. If handled well, they can be a beautiful addition to any document. Keep these things in mind when using them:

- Gradient fills are a good substitute for screened rectangles under text. You should keep them light if they will be placed underneath text. To insure readability— unless the screen is a very light color—it is not advisable to make a fill that goes from 100% to 0% and place text on it: the text would have to be reversed against the 100% and solid on the lighter part.

- You can create the appearance of a bleed without the expense of trimming your pages by using gradient fills that blend to white as they reach the edge of the page.

- One or more gradient fills placed on top of each other can be very effective.

Imported gradients

Gradient fills can be created as blends in programs such as FreeHand, Illustrator, PhotoStyler, or Photoshop. They can be set up as black and white or color blends. Here are some considerations when using them in PageMaker:

- There is the possibility of stepping or banding when using gradient fills, evidenced by visibly jumping from one shade to the next. Generally, the higher the resolution of your output, the less banding will be a problem.

- You cannot create high-quality gradient fills for use on a laser printer—banding is unavoidable.

- Gradient fills created in another software program and imported into PageMaker can be stretched or cropped. You must be careful, however; if you stretch a 1" original blend to a width of 3" or 4", the blend steps get larger. Sometimes this can result in the steps becoming visible.

Gradients without software

You can still produce gradient fills even if you do not have a scanner, drawing program, or other software to create them. It is possible to purchase self-adhesive sheets made by Letraset, Zipatone, or other manufacturers in art supply stores, and either paste them into your camera-ready art boards or provide them to your printer for stripping into film. They come in several dot sizes, with variable gradations.

Linking graphics files to your PageMaker document simplifies production. You can reduce the publication size by building links to the files it contains, and at the same time provide for automatic updating should those source files be changed.

Because PageMaker assembles files from numerous different programs in various file formats, it needs to maintain a link to the originals in order to prevent the publication from including all the data in the individual files.

Automatic Updating

Having graphics update automatically can be very useful. When a graphic is changed after it has been placed into a PageMaker file, the changes usually reflect a refinement that is desired: new information on a sales graph, color correction on a photograph, etcetera. As long as the original size and proportions of the graphic have not been changed, the link can be updated automatically and the revised graphic will retain all sizing, cropping, and other attributes that were assigned to it when first placed into PageMaker.

To make elements update automatically, choose Link options... under the Element menu. Check the box to Update automatically, and click OK. This enables you to select individual files that have been placed, and indicate whether they should update automatically by checking the box.

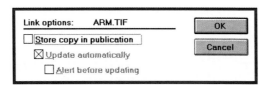

It is usually not desirable to have text files update automatically; this is because you can do formatting and editing of text within PageMaker after it has been placed—changing styles, alignment, and creating drop caps. If you were to choose automatic updating for a text file, when you reopen your PageMaker publication, it would find the original word-processed text document and use it to replace the refined and formatted version in your publication. This prevents making permanent changes to text files.

You should also check the Alert before updating option, in case you do not wish to have a specific file updated.

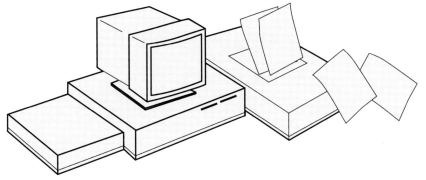

A PageMaker publication that is output and printed with minimal difficulty is the objective of the expert. The pages which follow contain information about files, output, and the printing process. Knowing as much as you can about these steps will enable you to make the right decisions for your layout.

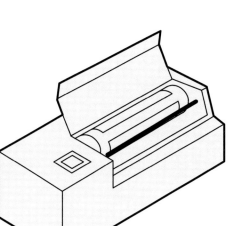

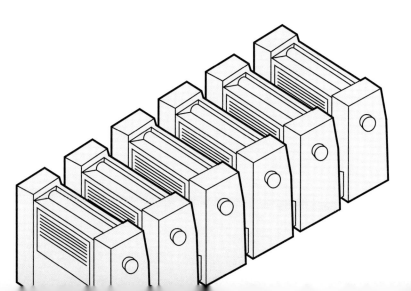

The maintenance and organization of electronic data files is the basis of all electronic publishing. It's sometimes frightening to realize that all your work on a given project is really nothing more than a series of lines of code represented by 0s and 1s. This makes it imperative to create PageMaker files that you and others can work with.

Storage and compression

File storage and compression are two of the most important issues confronting electronic publishers. Today's inexpensive storage media and faster, more effective ways to compress file sizes make complex data files possible—and usable.

PageMaker files can become very large, very fast, because PageMaker assembles data files generated in other programs. A full-color TIFF scan can contain many megabytes of information. When you place several scans into your document along with EPS and text files, the PageMaker file can very quickly exceed the capacity of your available storage media. PageMaker helps alleviate this situation by enabling you to link images to a publication. This is one reason why it's important to link images to the PageMaker file rather than including the graphic or scan in the document itself.

If floppy disks can't hold your file, you will need to consider other forms of storage media to transfer files to service bureaus for output. Other storage media available include SyQuest cartridges (44 or 88 megabyte removable disks) or optical disks (600 megabyte removable cartridges) written to and read by special disk drives.

Compression programs such as PKZip by PK Ware. condense file size. These programs encode files so that they take up less space on disks. Sometimes a compression program can reduce a file to less than half of its original size. Compression programs are invaluable for sending large PageMaker files over modems to service bureaus or printers. Using a compression program can sometimes mean that a floppy disk is adequate to hold your file.

Generally, these products include a decompression program which you can distribute freely so that you can send compressed files to others without worry about whether they have the program or not. It is also possible to create what is called a self-extracting file, which decompresses automatically when it's double-clicked. However, these files are larger by necessity than the smallest compressed files.

Saving

When working with PageMaker files (or any files for that matter) it is essential to have backup copies because files can be accidentally deleted or even damaged. Many production departments are networked and backup takes place to a storage device on a nightly basis. Even this may not be often enough to make backups, especially if your working file is damaged at the end of a full day's work, before backup. My own rule of thumb is to make a backup copy after every four hours of work—and more often than that when a deadline is drawing near. Make backups of scans and other graphics files as well, because they too can become damaged.

It is important to establish work practices that are consistent and leave no room for doubt about which file is a backup and which is the current working file. It's sensible to keep current working files on your hard drive and make backup copies to floppy disks, SyQuest, or optical cartridges, or to the network server.

Here is a system of making backup files that will also compact the document size:

1. Save the file using Save As.... The current publication name such as MYFILE.PM5, is already shown in the file name box. Click OK. PageMaker will ask you if you want to replace the file. Click OK. This compacts the file.

2. Choose Save As... again, and type in a new file name, replacing the last three characters of the file name (not the extension) with _BU. for example, if you file is called REPORT.PM5, name the copy you are about the save REPOR_BU.PM5. Do not change the file extension (the .PM5) or PageMaker will not see the file in the Open dialog box. Click OK.

3. After the copy is saved, close the publication. Use File Manager to copy the backup file to the backup disk. Avoid saving the copy directly to the backup disk. While this is safe with some backup media such as Syquesxt drives, it is not recommended to save directly to floppy disks.

Organization and naming

If you do a large amount of work for the same client, or have several related projects going on at the same time, file and folder organization and naming can be organized as follows:

1. Create a master folder on your hard drive with a job number, followed by the client or project name. (An easy way to assign job numbers is by a six digit process beginning with year, followed by month, and then by the numerical order of the job. For example, the second job in April of 1994 would be numbered 940402.)

2. Inside the master folder, create three other folders: Text (if you are receiving word-processed files for placement into your publication), Graphics (to hold scans, screen captures, and other art files), and Final, (to hold your current working PageMaker publications).

3. Place text and graphics files in the proper folders, and save working files to the Final folder. Use job numbers in the file names if you wish (to facilitate finding the files later when revisions need to be made to the publication.)

4. As you complete projects, archive them to backup media. Storing them on your hard drive after they are completed can be a waste of disk space, and will slow down processing time for your CPU.

5. You can create a database in a program such as FileMaker Pro including information such as job number, date, file names, commercial printer, color numbers, and so forth to keep track of where these files are located and the necessary information about them.

Printers

The destination printer for your files determines many design and production decisions. From a flyer printed on a laser printer, to a full-color brochure requiring high-resolution imagesetting, understanding your printing options will help you determine the best way to accommodate your printer in your design work.

Dot Matrix printers

Dot matrix printers should be used for final output of low-end publications such as personal correspondence and the like. Resolution from a dot matrix printer is not adequate to justify the cost of any reproduction method other than photocopy.

Inkjet printers

In terms of quality, inkjet printers are better than dot matrix, but not as good as laser printers. Though their resolution is sometimes comparable to or higher than that of laser printers, the method used for placing the dots on the page is less precise.

Inkjet printers are useful for producing color proofs, but are not recommended for documents to be reproduced by the offset printing process.

Laser printers

Laser printers were crucial in the desktop publishing revolution. Many people believe that all desktop published documents are laser printed: most are proofed on a laser printer, and some never go beyond laser printer stage.

Laser printers have lower resolution than imagesetters. The resolution of most laser printers is 300 dots per inch (DPI), although some can achieve output as high as 1,000 DPI. The higher the DPI, the sharper the type and images in your publication.

Laser prints are not generally used as camera ready art for offset printing. Because of their low resolution, they print acceptable announcements, flyers, letters, and other such projects. The fact that they cannot print to the edge of a page means that bleeds are not possible (unless you're printing a letter-sized page on a printer capable of tabloid sized output).

Color laser printing

Color laser technology has yielded some very high-end color printers that can be used for both proofing and to produce the final printed piece, especially for signs or posters that will be produced in limited quantities. Many companies are now offering color copiers that you can combine with a raster image processor (RIP) that output high-quantity color PageMaker documents. Current limitations of this technology include low resolution, small page size, and inability to print a two-sided page. These limitations are being rapidly addressed by manufacturers, and in the future you can expect to see many laser printed color publications, that were never output to film or plate.

Oversize printing

For creating signs, posters, oversize proofs and comps, many service bureaus offer large format printers that output PostScript files at very large sizes—measured in feet, not inches. Although color quality is not outstanding, the technology should improve steadily until this method becomes an accepted standard for the creation of signs. Look for output under such names as Cactus or Megachrome when contacting service bureaus.

Imagesetters

When there's talk of high resolution film or positive output, it's usually about "Lino." This refers to the Linotronic imagesetter built by the Linotype-Hell Corporation, a standard, along with other brands of high-resolution printers such as Agfa Compugraphic and Varityper. These printers are capable of output over 3,000 DPI, and are usually only found in large companies or service bureaus because of their cost.

Imagesetter output can usually be purchased from service bureaus for a few dollars per letter size page. It can be ordered either on paper or film (positive or negative). There are a number of things to know about ordering high-resolution imagesetting, which are covered in the Service Bureaus section, page 165.

Printing PostScript

Windows uses a set of graphical instructions called the Graphical Device Interface of GDI, to draw everything that you see on the monitor. When printing to a PostScript device, these GDI instructions must be converted to their PostScript equivalents. In PageMaker 5.0 this is accomplished by PageMaker.

PostScript, a page description language developed by Adobe Systems, has become the standard for printing pages composed on personal computers. Printer manufacturers license the software from Adobe for their PostScript printers. Some printers, called PostScript clones, have interpreters that emulate PostScript code, but this does not always work flawlessly.

If you wish to output a PageMaker page on a PostScript printer at another location, such as a service provider's Imagesetter, you can save the PageMaker file as pure PostScript code.

PostScript printer description files (PPDs)

PPDs are only used for PostScript printers. They come with PageMaker 5.0, and you select the ones to add to your System folder when you install PageMaker. There is no need to install PPDs for printers you do not have. Each PPD contains detailed information about a specific printer including paper sizes, default fonts, optimized screen angles, and more. PageMaker uses PPDs to efficiently print to specific printers.

PostScript and TrueType fonts

The Macintosh uses both TrueType and PostScript fonts.

PostScript fonts are made up of two parts: bitmapped fonts and the printer font file. The bitmapped fonts are used for screen display, and the printer font files are interpreted by the printer to produce a proper typeface.

TrueType is Apple's System 7 font solution used to display scaled typefaces without the jagged edges often seen onscreen. They also allow non-PostScript printers to print the typefaces at any size while maintaining their sharp images.

When PageMaker files are sent for imagesetting, use of TrueType fonts can produce unpredictable results.

Downloading fonts

When you use a font that is not installed in your laser printer, the Macintosh must download the PostScript font file to the printer. This takes time, and can significantly slow down the printing process. If there is a font that you will use often, download that font to your printer using the font downloader that comes with the font package. You cannot do this with too many fonts, however, because your printer has limited memory.

It is possible in many cases to attach an additional hard drive to a printer and download additional fonts to that drive so the printer can use it as memory.

Printer utilities

■ **Adobe Type Manager (ATM)**

■ **Adobe Type Reunion**

■ **Suitcase**

Printing PostScript to disk

This is a method of creating a file for output if the output system does not have Page-Maker, or for creating "snapshots" of individual pages for inclusion into a PageMaker or other document.

In earlier versions of PageMaker, color files had to be saved as OPI PostScript and opened into Aldus PrePrint to create full color separations. Color separation can now be done without PrePrint, so there is less need to generate PostScript files from Pagemaker.

If you do wish to perform this function for sending a complete file for output, it is done simply, using the Print dialog box.

1. Choose Print under the File menu.

2. Make all selections, such as page numbers to be printed, and so forth.

3. When finished, click the Options button, and check the option Write PostScript to file.

4. Click the Normal button.

5. Click Save as… or Save. Save as… will give you the option of giving the PostScript file a different name and location.

To save a file as a PostScript (EPS) graphic, such as the reduced page displayed here, follow steps 1-3 above, and in step 4, click EPS rather than Normal.

Printers

Printing PostScript

Windows uses a set of graphical instructions called the Graphical Device Interface of GDI, to draw everything that you see on the monitor. When printing to a PostScript device, these GDI instructions must be converted to their PostScript equivalents. In PageMaker 5.0 this is accomplished by PageMaker.

PostScript, a page description language developed by Adobe Systems, has become the standard for printing pages composed on personal computers. Printer manufacturers license the software from Adobe for their PostScript printers. Some printers, called PostScript clones, have interpreters that emulate PostScript code, but this does not always work flawlessly.

If you wish to output a PageMaker page on a PostScript printer at another location, such as a service provider's Imagesetter, you can save the PageMaker file as pure PostScript code.

PostScript printer description files (PPDs)

PPDs are only used for PostScript printers. They come with PageMaker 5.0, and you select the ones to add to your System folder when you install PageMaker. There is no need to install PPDs for printers you do not have. Each PPD contains detailed information about a specific printer including paper sizes, default fonts, optimized screen angles, and more. PageMaker uses PPDs to efficiently print to specific printers.

PostScript and TrueType fonts

The Macintosh uses both TrueType and PostScript fonts.

PostScript fonts are made up of two parts: bitmapped fonts and the printer font file. The bitmapped fonts are used for screen display, and the printer font files are interpreted by the printer to produce a proper typeface.

TrueType is Apple's System 7 font solution used to display scaled typefaces without the jagged edges often seen onscreen. They also allow non-PostScript printers to print the typefaces at any size while maintaining their sharp images.

When PageMaker files are sent for imagesetting, use of TrueType fonts can produce unpredictable results.

Downloading fonts

When you use a font that is not installed in your laser printer, the Macintosh must download the PostScript font file to the printer. This takes time, and can significantly slow down the printing process. If there is a font that you will use often, download that font to your printer using the font downloader that comes with the font package. You cannot do this with too many fonts, however, because your printer has limited memory.

It is possible in many cases to attach an additional hard drive to a printer and download additional fonts to that drive so the printer can use it as memory.

Printer utilities

■ **Adobe Type Manager (ATM)**

■ **Adobe Type Reunion**

■ **Suitcase**

160

This "snapshot" of the facing page was saved as an EPS graphic by writing PostScript to disk, and imported into the PageMaker file. It was reduced in size, and the rectangle and drop shadow defining its edges were added with PageMaker's graphics tools.

Service bureaus

Service bureaus produce high resolution imagesetting of your electronic files. This enables you to provide camera ready art to a commercial printer. The key to working successfully with a service bureau is to exchange information about their policies, prices, turnaround time, software and hardware, and specifics about your material.

Range of services

Service bureaus offer different services—most of which center around high-resolution imagesetting. Some are open 24 hours a day with self-service workstations to create or polish your files, then print to laser printers or imagesetters. These service bureaus often include access to scanners and color printers, and on-site high volume photocopying. Other bureaus do not offer this kind of direct customer involvement, and specialize in high-end scanning, color proofs, and image-setting supervised by well-trained and knowledgeable staff—usually at a higher cost per page. If you have not worked with scanning or imagesetting before, it is probably best to use a full-service shop. As you become more familiar with the processes, self-service may become a viable alternative for you.

Some companies opened from the onset of electronic publishing throughout the late 1980s. Others evolved as expanded services from traditional typesetting or prepress houses. The latter is usually better for high-end color publishing requirements because they have more experience in traditional typography and color separation standards, and use a traditional method when it makes sense to do so.

Scheduling

Electronic publishing is a deadline-driven business. Both self- and full-service shops are often hectic places with a high level of activity. For this reason, it may be unrealistic to expect them to drop everything else to meet your deadline when you need a few pages of imagesetter output immediately. Build service bureau turnaround time into your deadline and budget. Many companies can accommodate quick turnaround with 1 hour, 2 hour, or 8 hour service—and charge from double to quadruple for doing so. Your deadline may require rush service, and you must be prepared to pay for it.

Make appointments at self-service shops, and build in time for things to go wrong, because they often do. Alert full-service shops to when they can expect to receive your files, how many pages you'll be printing, and when you need them. Again, even with full-service output, build in time for mistakes, because they can happen.

Before sending files

Never send your original file. Make a copy of it and send the copy.

Never send a file for imagesetting until you have seen a final laser proof. Skipping this simple step can cost you frustration and money. Send laser proofs of each page with your order. Someone running imagesetter output late at night has no way of knowing if what's being imaged is correct, unless there's a laser print to compare to.

162

If you cannot get your laser printer to print a file, don't send it to a service bureau and expect them to "fix" it. This will cause them to waste time, and they may charge you. If you can't get your file to print, don't make the assumption that they will be able to.

Make sure your file is exactly the way it needs to be. Service bureaus are very reluctant to open your files and make changes to them. Do not ask them to do so, unless you have a long-standing relationship with the company and know their capabilities.

Transport media

The enormous file sizes of many PageMaker projects often make the traditional floppy disk unworkable when transmitting files for imagesetting.

If you use a file compression program, make sure that your service bureau has the specific program you're using, and can decompress your file. Otherwise, be sure to send a self-extracting file.

When sending a SyQuest disk or optical cartridge, make sure that the service bureau has a drive to handle your removable disk. Put the files you want to have output into a readily visible directory. Don't send a disk with other valuable original files on it, unless they are backed up. These disks are very expensive, so clearly label them with your name, address, and telephone number.

This order form from Octagon Graphics of San Francisco shows how many questions must be answered when ordering imagesetter output.

Modem transmission

Modems are another way to get files to service bureaus. Many shops have computers set aside to receive modem transmissions from their customers, some with easy-to-use bulletin-board interfaces. If your file is really large, you should compress it before sending. If you don't have a compression program, simply let the transmission take as long as it needs—providing you and your service bureau are willing to tie up the phone lines and computers for that long. You can send large files at night after you've left the office, but be aware that if there is a transmission error, you'll return in the morning only to find an interrupted modem transmission message.

Information for service bureaus

Most service bureaus have developed order forms with an extensive checklists to deal with the information about particular files and the specific kinds of output customers require. If you do not have one of these checklists, you should still provide this information to your service bureau. (See order form from previous page.) Some of the questions contained on these lists are as follows:

■ File names

The importance of this information is obvious; this is how the service bureau knows what file(s) to image. Be sure to include the names of any necessary linked files, too.

■ File type

The service bureau needs to know which software program and what version of the program you have used in creating your file(s).

■ Page size and orientation

The service bureau needs to know whether your file is letter size, tabloid size or larger to provide the proper output.

■ Output characteristics

The output you need is specified here. Do you want film or paper, positive or negative, emulsion up or down?

■ Line screens

Whether you are providing your printer with film negative or positive output, you must be aware of the line screen requirements. (For more information on line screens, see Image Control, page 146.) Many service bureaus will provide a default line screen of 90 or 100 if you do not specify.

■ Linked files

If you have included linked graphics in your publication, electronic files of those graphics must be provided so that the data contained in them is available to Page-Maker for the final output process. It is your responsibility to make sure that all files are provided and properly linked to the images in your publication. You must also assign line screen values for any grayscale TIFF images, or they will not print properly.

■ Fonts

Knowing the fonts contained in a file is crucial for the service bureau, for the same fonts must be on the system that outputs your page(s). You must indicate all fonts used (don't forget Zapf Dingbats, fonts used in logos or graphics, or other incidental fonts). If the service bureau does not have the fonts you've used, send along electronic files of screen and printer fonts for them.

Utilities are beginning to appear that claim to create suitable substitute fonts for output by matching the closest available font and changing its characteristics to approximate those you originally used. This might be useful in a pinch, but in general, should be avoided.

Compiling file information

Few frustrations in electronic publishing are worse than finding a Yen sign where you expected bullets because of a font substitution on twenty-four pages of imagesetter film. A mistake like this usually requires rerunning all the film at rush rates. Fortunately, there is an easy and automatic way to compile most of the information a service bureau needs about your file. It's the Aldus Addition Display pub info... feature. Here's how it works:

1. Run the "Display pub info..." Addition from the Aldus Additions submenu under Utilities.

2. Click "Save".

3. You can print the information file out for reference, or to be sent to your service bureau.

Service bureau equipment

Electronic prepress service bureaus are built around output of high-resolution image-setting. Using the Linotronic imagesetter as an example, this is what high-resolution equipment consists of:

■ **Raster image processor (RIP)**

The RIP is the heart of the system. It is a computer with a very fast CPU and a large amount of memory. It contains the PostScript interpreter that converts PostScript code to the high resolution bitmap needed by the imaging recorder.

■ **Imaging recorder**

This is the part of the imagesetter that actually prints onto the film or paper. The feed mechanisms of these recorders must be very precise to maintain registration for each printout.

■ **Processor**

After the film or paper inside the imagesetter is printed, it must be processed. This is similar to developing film from cameras; it requires a darkroom process to create the image. Service bureaus that regularly clean and calibrate their developers offer better quality, and this is something you should inquire about.

Other equipment

Your service bureau may have some of the following equipment:

■ **Scanners**

Scanners can be black and white or full color, with resolution up to 1,200 DPI or more. Some, such as the Barneyscan enable you to scan slides or transparencies, and others can scan line art and continuous tone photographs. Drum scanners are high-end equipment requiring art to be attached to a drum that spins as the scanning takes place. If you send art to a service bureau to be scanned, be sure to specify resolution, file type, and format. Make sure art you send is well-protected and labelled, and send along enough disk storage to contain the scans that are sent back to you.

Some service bureaus offer scanners equipped with optical character recognition (OCR) software that converts printed or typewritten text into a word-processing file that can be edited on your computer and placed into PageMaker.

■ **Color proofing systems**

Color proofs can be very useful when checking the quality of the color, and verifying separations. Some color printers, such as the IRIS or Canon Color Laser printers image directly from your file. Others, such as 3M MatchPrint or DuPont Chromalin use the actual film separations for generating color proofs.

Types of output

Speak to your commercial printer to find out what type of output is required for your project. It will fall into these categories:

■ **Paper output**

High resolution paper output of your files can be used when reproducing by photocopy, for proofing purposes, for instances when you will be physically pasting artwork onto the boards before submitting them to a commercial printer, and for offset printing. When you provide paper output to a printer, it is still necessary to shoot film from the art, resulting in another generation, and subtle degradation of type and art.

■ **Film output**

For commercial printing you almost always want film output because it provides the clearest, sharpest printing. There are some difficulties when working with film—especially negatives, to be aware of. One of the most difficult areas concerns final proofing. Everything is a reverse, and what's supposed to print black displays clear. This can be confusing, especially when reversed type and/or gray tones are involved. About the only way to proof negatives is to use a light table, or tape them up on a window.

You need to know whether to provide film positives or negatives. Usually, negatives are the correct choice, but this is a matter to be discussed with your printer. Also ask whether emulsion side should be up or down.

Aldus has three additional programs that work with PageMaker to produce output. They are TrapWise, PressWise, and PrePrint.

Aldus TrapWise

Trapping is a color printing process that compensates for potential misregistration as the paper passes through a printing press. Without trapping, printed output may have slight gaps between color elements allowing the underlying paper stock to show through. With trapping, however, the edges of color objects are enlarged or reduced just enough to cover any gaps that may occur.

TrapWise automatically produces these traps by applying appropriate spreads and chokes to objects in color-conforming EPS files. Such files are generated by PostScript-language applications such as PageMaker, Aldus FreeHand, QuarkXPress, and Adobe Illustrator.

Once processed through TrapWise, the resulting EPS pages can be output to a PostScript compatible device, including imagesetters, platesetters, and printing presses.

TrapWise handles complex trapping situations such as graduated fills, very small text, and several intersecting colors. It is designed for use by professionals in service bureaus, prepress houses, commercial print shops, in-plant production departments, and publishing operations. It is not intended for the average PageMaker user.

Aldus PressWise

Imposition is the arrangement of pages for printing in a press form so that they will appear in correct order when the printed sheet is folded and trimmed. Aldus PressWise is an advanced page-imposition program that enables prepress operators to automatically prepare multipage documents for printing, folding, and binding in the correct page order. Professional film strippers and production artists use PressWise to design templates for specific imposition needs.

PressWise has automated features to convert the pages of a PostScript file created in PageMaker into precise signature forms.

A good way to understand imposition is to actually take a sheet of paper, fold it, number it, and make up an eight-page signature as described below:

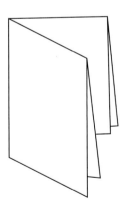

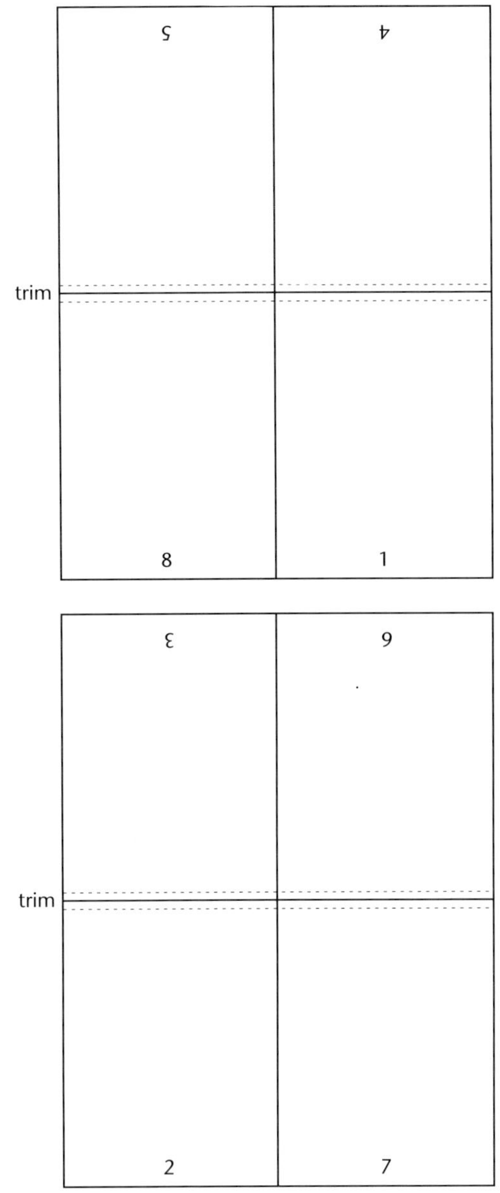

```
┌─────────────┬─────────────┐
│      5      │      4      │
│             │             │
│             │             │
trim ········ │ ············ │
│             │             │
│      8      │      1      │
└─────────────┴─────────────┘

┌─────────────┬─────────────┐
│      3      │      6      │
│             │             │
│         .   │             │
trim ········ │ ············ │
│             │             │
│      2      │      7      │
└─────────────┴─────────────┘
```

The diagram to the left shows how a printed 8-page signature is folded. The diagram above shows the imposition arrangement of the individual pages prior to printing.

Aldus PrePrint

Previous versions of PageMaker required that you transfer your publication to a Macintosh and use Aldus PrePrint to generate CMYK color separations. This is no longer necessary with PageMaker 5.0, although there are still times when PrePrint must be used:

■ If you have used RGB TIFF images in your publication, you will need to use PrePrint to separate. CMYK TIFF images can be separated directly by PageMaker.

■ If you use Aldus PressWise to create a layout imposition, later find it must be color separated.

■ To enhance any continuous tone images included in your publication.

Before using PrePrint, create a PostScript file for separations in PageMaker. Pay special attention to the printing options you select to ensure that linked files and scanned graphics are available, the right PPD file is selected, and all the fonts for printing text within EPS graphics are available.

The capabilities of commercial printers can vary more than those of service bureaus. You must find the right printer for any project, balancing criteria such as quality of previous work, price, turnaround time, and service. It is crucial to know different printers in your area and to build good relationships with them. Their work is the final step in your PageMaker projects.

Different capabilities

Commercial printers can be classified by the kind of work they do. Some specialize in high-volume, and they do print runs of at least 50,000 units; others gladly accept low-volume four color runs. Some have huge web presses larger than semi trailers, while others run small sheet-fed presses that can be quickly and easily set up for two or four color sheet fed work. There are quick printers and high quality printers, and everything in between. A quick printer I have used for years has consistently provided low-cost, fast, high-quality full-color work, so you can't make assumptions about capabilities.

Printers are almost always willing to visit your location, talk about their capabilities, and show you their work. They also are usually very happy to give you a tour of their facility.

Prepress departments

Some large printing companies maintain full service prepress departments and are capable of taking PageMaker files on disk. (Soon, direct-to-plate technology will be perfected that will make film output unnecessary.) Having files output by the printer saves you the expense of using a service bureau. Of course, the printer is going to be much more likely to output files the way they are needed for printing.

By now, most printers are familiar with electronic publishing, and if you work with them from the beginning of a project, they can give you the benefit of their experience and many valuable tips.

Getting quotes

When securing bids or prices for printing, it's important to get quotes from more than one company. If you're working for a client, your client will appreciate (and maybe even require) this thoroughness. It can be time consuming, so it's convenient to use a system that makes the process easy for everyone concerned.

Create a form to be used for printing quotes with fill-in-the-blank information about a specific job. Fill in the form with the specifics for your job, make photocopies, and fax the form to different printers for quotes. (Let the printers know it is coming.) This helps the printers to quickly return quotes, in writing, of the cost.

Don't be impatient if it takes a printer two or three days to get a quote back to you. They need to price paper and assess available resources before they can give you an accurate price and turnaround time. For this reason, it is important to get printing quotes and to decide on the printer early in the design process.

Some of the things a printer needs to know about your job are:

- Number of copies
- 1- or 2-sided
- 1-, 2-, or 4-color
- ink coverage (light or heavy)
- bleeds
- finished size
- folds
- trims
- binding
- turnaround time
- type of camera ready art
- paper stock
- die cuts
- foil stamping

Meeting deadlines

Printers are busy people; they are the final step in a process of deadlines. Everyone wants their work printed right away, and people often expect printers to make up deadlines that may have been missed by copywriters, designers, and service bureaus. Printers will work with you on deadlines, but there are certain processes—such as time for ink to dry before work can be folded—that cannot be shortened.

Printers are schedule jugglers. They have expensive equipment that must be kept in operation. When you are going to miss a deadline for getting work to them, it is only fair to give them as much notice as possible. This kind of communication will help in building and maintaining good relationships with printers.

Bluelines, color proofs, and press checks

Even if you are working under a tight deadline, it is important not to skip the proofing process at the commercial printing stage. There are several ways for you to proof work before it has been printed.

■ Bluelines

Bluelines are proofs that a printer creates from film before it is made into printing plates. They show the position of all elements, and are usually trimmed and mocked up in the same way as the final document. There is usually a charge for creating a blueline—and it is well worth the cost. You can spot imperfections the printer may miss like scratches and similar irregularities, misalignment or bad trim information. You may also pick up an error you missed when you were proofing film. This gives you a chance to run new film before that error is repeated in 25,000 copies.

■ Color proofs

3M Matchprints or DuPont Chromalins are used to proof process color jobs, to ensure that alignment, color, and all other aspects of the job are correct. While they are relatively expensive, they are cheaper than the cost of rerunning an entire job because of a mistake that could have been corrected.

■ Press checks

Press checks are often difficult to schedule; however, they are invaluable, especially for process color runs. At a press check, you can see one of the first pieces run off, and ensure that everything is correct. You can stop the presses if something is wrong; while that's not a pleasant prospect, it's better than rejecting a job after it's printed. There will usually be an extra charge for a press check.

Post-press services

Printing your publication isn't the end of the process at the commercial printer. There are also the issues of binding, trimming, folding, die cutting, packaging, and delivery. Ensure that you build in the time needed for these things to happen. Some specialties, such as die cutting, may be jobbed out to others.

Index

W

X–Z